MW00799547

Through Our Eyes

Poetry and Prompts

Compiled by
Courtenay Nold and Travis Partington

Through Our Eyes

Eyes

Poetry and Prompts

Compiled by
Courtenay Nold and Travis Partington

Southern Arizona Press
Sierra Vista, Arizona

of Indiana, Inc.
Helping Veterans And Families

Helping Veterans And Families (HVAF) helps homeless Veterans return to self-sufficiency and engages at-risk Veterans and their families to prevent them from becoming homeless by providing supportive housing, case management, employment support, therapy, and basic needs including food, hygiene, and clothing. Each year, HVAF provides over 33,000 services to 1,200+ Veterans. HVAF of Indiana houses, supports, and advocates for all Veterans and their families to help them achieve the best possible quality of life. Their vision: hope, housing and self-sufficiency for all Veterans and their families.

Through Our Eyes

Compiled by Courtenay Nold and Travis Partington

First Edition

Content Copyright © 2023 by Courtenay Nold & Travis Partington

All rights reserved.

Except as permitted under the Copyright Act of 1976, no portion of this book may be reproduced or distributed in any form, or by any means without prior written consent of the individual authors or the publisher. Individual works Copyright © retained by the poetic author. Previously published works have been cited and each publication acknowledged to the best of our ability. If any citations have been missed, such errors will be corrected in subsequent reprints.

Editor: Courtenay Nold and Travis Partington
Poetic Prompts by: Travis Partington
Formatting: Southern Arizona Press
Cover Design: Courtenay Nold
Cover Art: Image by Grae Dickason from Pixabay
Used under Pixabay Content License
Poets photos Copyright © retained by submitting poets

Published by Southern Arizona Press
Sierra Vista, Arizona 85635
www.SouthernArizonaPress.com

ISBN: 978-1-960038-43-2

Poetry, Self-help, Veterans, First Responders

Foreword

Robert Willoughby, Psy. D.

Trauma comes in many forms, shapes, and sizes. It affects all people regardless of gender, age, race, job, religion, culture, and lifestyle. Courtenay Nold is doing great work by compiling these poems in Through Our Eyes representing individuals' poetry, experiences of trauma, and Post-Traumatic Stress Disorder (PTSD). It is a beautiful work lending support to the HVAF of Indiana. It serves as inspiration to the reader through engaging with the thoughts, and creativity of others and providing insight into emotion.

In this work Courtenay represents the poetry of military Veterans and others associated with high levels of trauma. Trauma exposure is ubiquitous in the line of work for these professions and can develop into PTSD or other stress related challenges. These works are elements of healing, release, and aspects of creativity that include emotions and thoughts that help one to grow.

Courtenay has been kind enough to encourage some of my poetry reflecting aspects of trauma. My experience comes from 15 years as a paramedic engaging with trauma of all types. I unfortunately saw some devastating effects of this exposure on my colleagues. This poem represents some of the emotional blowbacks and experiences one may have as they engage with and experience the aftereffects of trauma.

WALKING ON EGGSHELLS

Can't say it is an absolute willing choice, more of a survival tactic.
A choice, but one between perceived death, damage, or destruction
   vs. self-preservation.
Trying to walk gently. Though, most often, the shells crack.
Then onto fight/flight/freeze.
A seemingly never-ending cycle.
Always aware, prepared for danger, waiting-hypervigilant.
Can I ever break this cycle?

Can I be free of the persistent worry; The looming sense of
   foreboding, the distrust of others.
The negative thoughts and deprecating self-views, the intrusive
   thoughts, and nightmares?
How long can I avoid the triggers, the flashbacks, the anger?
Oh, that ever-present anger Is there a way to escape?
Choose flight into that fateful final decision of the void?
Or will that lead to eternal damnation?
Do I care at this point?

I do care.

And dammit there are other choices than the corner I have allowed
   myself to be painted into!
I can choose to draw boundaries. Say F##k You!!! to the pain and
   definitely the abuser(s).
I can choose to live.

While I am not the perpetrator, I, for sure, can choose to help myself heal!
I can choose growth and resilience!
I can do it for me!!! I can choose me! I can choose me! I can choose me!
I do choose me!

In choosing me, I can offer you a better me!!!

I choose me!!!

Musings from a trauma survivor

RSW

A life of trauma was something well understood by Viktor Frankl, a Holocaust survivor, Psychiatrist, and writer. He experienced the horrors of the camps, lost his family, and lost many friends (Frankl, 1959/2006). Through it all he kept looking forward and working to develop meaning and show others meaning in their lives and suffering. He created Logotherapy, a style of therapy designed to help the patient develop meaning of events and their lives (Frankl, 1959/2006). In being able to create a sense of meaning encourages a sense of belonging and a sense of purpose. To know your life has meaning is very valuable.

"The cave you fear to enter holds the treasure you seek."

This quote is often attributed to Joseph Campbell, an American writer and comparative mythologist. While not found in his works, it is most likely a distillation of his thoughts (https://quoteinvestigator.com/2013/05/23/campbell-treasure/). It is an apt quote in representing our difficulty with emotions. It is often difficult for many to engage with their own emotions and even to understand them. Once we create that understanding we create a deeper sense of self and open the door to adding meaning to our lives as emotions serve as guides toward purpose, meaning and even a sense of fulfillment.

Brene' Brown identifies the challenges of understanding emotions in her work Atlas of the Heart: Mapping meaningful connection and the language of human experience (Brown, 2022). Brown is an adept researcher who can take her results and adapt them to applicability and understanding in our daily lives. In her work she has identified that out of 87 different emotions most people identify three: happiness, sadness, and anger (Brown, 2022). Brown (2022) further develops the aspects of anger as being used frequently due to the ease and due to many emotions being subsumed under anger, which is often regarded as a secondary emotion. Brown (2022) encourages us to engage with more emotions like empathy, compassion, and gratitude, and encourages us to be vulnerable to experience our strength and develop meaning in our lives. Indeed, the more we understand about ourselves the more engaged with our emotions we can be, the better we can guide ourselves and experience the highs and lows meaningfully.

Recognition of thoughts, emotions, and being seen are important aspects of the journey with trauma, PTSD, and creating understanding for those with that experience. This journey is mired in a history of stigma toward those suffering with PTSD being branded as yellow, cowards, or other negative epithets. In truth, to be able to endure the symptoms of PTSD shows a great deal of strength (Willoughby, 2021).

It is important to note the presence of stigma as it limits public understanding of PTSD and puts a negative shadow on the experience which can drive some away from treatment. It can encourage negative views of the self or others. Early perspectives did not include a significant concern for mental health and were geared toward a strictly strength-based view seeing those suffering as weak or defective. Stigma interferes with treatment seeking due to fears of embarrassment, worries of peers persecuting them or treating them differently, being seen as weak or seen as lesser than, fear of being blamed, and/or damage to reputation (Hom et al.,2018).

The symptoms of PTSD are intricate and unique to everyone. They come from exposure to trauma(s) such as war, battle, abuse, rape, sexual abuse, car accidents, witnessing death or events leading to death, racism, adversity against diverse populations, and natural disasters; hurricanes, tornados, earthquakes, severe storms, tidal waves that bring about severe loss, death, and a fear of losing one's life (American Psychiatric Association, 2013). There are arguably others, though this is a comprehensive list. These types of events impact a sense of safety with very real fears of a loss of life or in some cases a sense of freedom. Suicide is an unfortunate reality that is a maladaptive coping skill that is used in response to the pain and suffering associated with PTSD, stress, and trauma exposure (Willoughby, 2021). It is a signifier that we all need to keep developing our understanding and continue to work to help those in need. It is a resounding reason for the importance of this work, these poems, and the dedication to supporting Veterans.

PTSD symptoms include intrusive memories (flashbacks, nightmares of events, unwanted memories), avoidance (isolation, withdrawal, pushing others away, avoiding dealing with thoughts, feelings, and emotions, avoiding places or people associated with trauma), negative changes in thinking and mood, and changes in physical and emotional reactions. (American Psychiatric Association, 2013). These are experienced in various ways and can include aspects of depression, anxiety, depersonalization, and dissociation.

To put this into perspective, a Veteran Soldier, including First Responders, can experience a flashback that puts them in the experience of being in an exposure event like a battle in which they feel the same feelings and impacts to safety and may even feel there is a threat to their life. Such experiences serve to destabilize an individual and make it hard to engage in daily life leading to withdrawal. A Soldier may also wake in the middle of the night screaming about losing their best friend in a firefight while right next to them. In EMS related experiences, a paramedic may avoid an intersection where a bad accident occurred, avoid driving by a house where they had performed CPR on a child and lost them, or woke up from a nightmare of not being able to save a spouse on Christmas Day.

Pain and suffering are common things to see in EMS, First Responders and Soldiers/Veterans. In the work we are exposed to much tragedy. As much as we may not want to be affected by it, we all are. This poem reflects some associated thought processes.

PAIN AND SUFFERING, WHAT HAVE YOU DONE TO ME?

Pain and suffering, what have you done to me?
Death, loss, hurt, and illness are the things I see.
Is that a young child crying on the bed?
Did someone smack her in the head?

I did CPR last night.
It was on a child in a plight.
I cannot forget the sight.
Did someone lead her to the light?

One more hour and I get to go home.
To rest like a pharaoh in a tomb.
But what is that I hear?
The black box yelling can you clear.

Another call you see.
My job never done a life chosen by you and me.
Chest pain one Nitro down.
Update, CPR in progress as we race through town.

Grandmother maybe it was not meant to be.
I am sorry we did all we could you see.
Some say god's will it be.
I cry with her and listen to her plea.

Beautiful child why do you shoot these drugs
They do not provide lasting comfort.
What you need is some love and hugs
Not bad drugs, Narcan and life support

Pain and injury, suffering we see.
Guns pulled, shots fired, insults hurled at me.
This life of service and sacrifice
Wears on me, what a small paycheck does it suffice?

RSW

Treatment for PTSD includes many forms of therapy including talk therapy, cognitive behavioral therapy (CBT), dialectical behavior therapy (DBT), trauma focused cognitive behavior therapy (TF-CBT), psychodynamic therapies, eye movement desensitization and reprocessing (EMDR), narrative therapy, cognitive processing therapy (CPT), exposure therapies, and medication assisted therapies (van der Kolk, 2014). There are also current trials using micro doses of MDMA, and others. Bessel Van Der Kolk (2014) identified many adjunctive therapies that can help in his work The Body Keeps the Score. These include Yoga, Tai Chi, meditation, Qi Gong, drama/theater, and other accessible activities (van der Kolk, 2014). An experience with Shakespearian plays was interesting in its ability to help the participants process their trauma (van der Kolk, 2014). This brings us to poetry.

Creative arts including poetry are therapies that one can do at home or on the go. It does not require a therapist, though one could incorporate it into their therapy and use it to explore their thoughts and feelings with a therapist. Some poetry is obvious as to the message, thoughts and feelings that are present while some is not as obvious, and can be subtle, representative, or intricate. Brené Brown's (2022) research shows how important creativity can be in identifying and experiencing emotions, a necessary component of healing, understanding the self, and making meaning of life. Poetry can help to recognize, process, understand, and resolve severe emotions thereby helping to heal trauma related impacts. My own research into the work of EMS, which included some Veterans turned EMTs or paramedics, identified the importance of creativity, the arts, reading, and expressive works as positive coping skills that helped participants manage stress in response to trauma exposure (Willoughby, 2021). This is further evidence of the necessity for expressive writing and creativity in our lives to serve our healing.

As you read through these pages, I would encourage you to note the experiences and emotions portrayed. The importance of the written word is palpable and the emotional expression very real. Writing out emotions has long been a great process of healing as therapists around the work encourage their clients to journal. Writing difficult experiences, thoughts, and emotions down is found to have a positive effect (Pennebaker & Smyth, 2019). Pennebaker & Smyth (2019) identified through their research that expressive writing can improve our physical health and our mental health. Simply by writing our experiences out we can reduce stress and improve our lives. They note that the effect is pronounced when writing about more difficult situations, and the effects lasted longer (Pennebaker & Smyth, 2019). This is another aspect of adding meaning through knowing and exploring our emotions as Brene' Brown (2022) encourages.

The poems in *'Through Our Eyes'* capture the feelings, experiences, thoughts, and journeys through their experiences on their journey through life. Prompts help to define some of the direction and enable the reader to take part and engage in the process on their own. Reading through, one will go on their own journey. As a creative art, poetry is interactive, and the reader becomes an integral part in the experience of the poem. On this journey you will learn about experiences that cause pain and suffering, processes of healing, see and feel warriors dig through struggle, identify strengths, and explore being victorious in their resilience. Lessons will be learned of being broken, picking up the pieces, and finding that inner strength in the face of loss. Perhaps you will learn that in making meaning of the journey, we can bring meaning and purpose to our lives as Viktor Frankl tells us we can in Man's Search for Meaning (Frankl, 1959/2006). Dig in, start this journey, and engage in the experiences and words so bravely shared by the warriors represented in these pages. Share their experiences and learn from their words and palpable presence. Explore life, and travel through some dark and some light times, understand struggle, and bring light in shared experience. Enjoy!

Stay Safe,

Robert Willoughby, Psy. D.

References:

American Psychiatric Association. (2013). *Diagnostic and statistical manual of mental disorders* (5th ed.). https://doi.org/10.1176/appi.books.9780890425596

Brown, B. (2022). *Atlas of the heart: Mapping meaningful connection and the language of human experience.* Random House Audio.

Frankl, V. (1959/2006). Man's search for meaning. Beacon Press.

Hom, M. A., Stanley, I. H., Spencer-Thomas, S., & Joiner, T. E. (2018). Mental health service
use and help-seeking among women firefighters with a career history of suicidality. *Psychological Services, 15*(3), 316–324. https://doi.org/10.1037/ser000020

Pennebaker, J. W., & Smyth, J. M. (2019). *Opening Up by Writing It Down: How Expressive Writing Improves Health and Eases Emotional Pain Third Edition.* Echo Point Books &amp: Media, LLC.

van der Kolk, B. (2014). *The body keeps the score: Brain, mind, and body in the healing of*
trauma. Penguin.

Willoughby, R. S. (2021). *A Heuristic Investigation of Private Ambulance Paramedics and EMTs* (Order No. 28869287). Available from Dissertations & Theses @ Michigan School of Psychology; Psychology Database. (2616651348). http://msp.idm.oclc.org/login?url=https://www.proquest.com/dissertations-theses/heuristic-investigation-private-ambulance/docview/2616651348/se-2

Table of Contents

Amarin Trichanh – Featured Poet

Poetry Prompt for 'Battle Scars'

Write a poem that portrays life as a battlefield, where every day is a relentless struggle. Reflect on the challenges and adversity faced and ask yourself what you have become in the midst of this ongoing conflict. Believe in your ability to overcome fear and perceive mistakes as your true adversaries. Explore the themes of resilience, self-discovery, and the determination to triumph over obstacles. Use powerful language, metaphor, and introspection to convey the inner and outer battles, as well as the unwavering spirit that drives you forward in your poetry.

BATTLE SCARS

The world is filled with wonders
Although life may not be kind
As we enter the battlefield we realize
Our lives are on the line

Every day is a constant struggle
Just to stay alive
In this deadly battlefield
Only the strong survives

Where is your battlefield
What are you fighting for
What have you overcome
While fighting these endless war

There will come a time
Where there will be endless nights
But the faith that's in our hearts
Will show us the light

Fear is our worst enemy
Battle that demon from within
Put on that armor and believe
That you will always win

We may become weary
And wounded 'til near death
Never cease, don't ever surrender
Until your last breath

And if the enemy is our mistakes
That leave some scars behind
May these be lessons learned
Let it be a sign

To become a stronger warrior
A reminder of why we fight
Or why we must keep moving
Before we start losing sight

Of the true meaning
Or what these wounds stand for
That just because we're wounded
Doesn't mean we lost the war

Society believes beauty is flawless
But these markings define
Inner beauty and strength
The legacy that's left behind

These wounds they tell stories
Of courage and survival too
From all aspect of life
We never even knew

Don't ever be ashamed
And hide your battle scars
It's your one legacy that defines
Who you really are

Your Writing Space

Amarin Trichanh – Featured Poet

Poetry Prompt for 'Never Giving Up on You'

Compose a poem that explores the profound connection between two individuals bound by love and life's challenges. One of them has fallen into darkness, haunted by inner demons, while the other's love shines brilliantly. Describe the struggle as the demons attempt to drag the one with the bright love into the abyss. Explore the themes of sacrifice, empathy, and the emotional toll of witnessing a loved one's descent into darkness. In the end, they both succumb to the same darkness, and tears are shed for the loss of both. Use evocative imagery, metaphor, and poignant language to convey the intensity of this emotional journey in your poetry.

NEVER GIVING UP ON YOU

Two hearts finally connected
Only to break apart
Memories too painful to forget
A void inside my heart

They say love conquers all
Deep down I still believe
Even with darkness and demons
I will not let them deceive

I knew it was only a matter of time
Now I finally see
That these demons have come
To take you away from me

Those eyes once filled with love
Have become less than kind
Your words turn into weapons
You were no longer mine

No matter how much I loved you
It made no difference at all
In the end I knew
I would lose and fall

I have fallen into that same darkness
Where I never wanted to be
Where I tried to save you from
So you can be with me

You have fought against me
While I was fighting for you
All of a sudden nothing matters
Nothing I say is true

It's not that I'm giving up
But a part of me has died
If you only knew
How many tears I've cried

I could never fight your demons
Just like you can't fight mine
I will always be the enemy
The one you will leave behind

So I call upon my angels
In this time of need
Take us through the storm
Through these dark hours indeed

The future is uncertain
People come and go
Although I may be distant
I thought you should know

One day you will understand
That true love never dies
You will be in my heart
I'm not saying good-bye

Your Writing Space

Amarin Trichanh – Featured Poet

Poetry Prompt for 'Shattered'

Write a poem that delves into the theme of betrayal and lies, examining how they can shatter the eyes, which are often seen as windows to one's soul. Explore the idea of trust being broken and the impact it has on the essence of a person. Describe the emotions and turmoil that arise when deceit is uncovered and the eyes that once held honesty and vulnerability are now clouded with pain and disillusionment. Use vivid imagery, metaphor, and expressive language to convey the profound transformation and the sense of loss in your poetry.

SHATTERED

If you were to seek the truth
By looking into someone's eyes
What if their souls were empty
And pain have silenced their cries

The windows to our souls
They don't always reveal
The truth and sometimes darkness
Take over what's real

Our body is a sacred temple
Home is in our hearts
When robbed and violated
Our existence falls apart

The most painful truth is when
Trust can get us killed
The heart grows dead and cold
So solid and still

Have you ever stared
Or seen those shattered eyes
Dripping bloody tears
From betrayal and lies?

Sometimes life is the very essence
That leaves us in the dark
The eyes that once light up the world
Have now lost all their sparks

The windows to our souls
They usually never lie
They tell stories and secrets
That we often hide

From the world without mercy
You can't reveal to much
Deception is too close for comfort
That leads to broken trust

Selfishness and greed
Lead us to destroy our own
Then in the hours of darkness
We're left all alone

Our souls are always hungry
We become more inhumane
Without remorse or hesitations
We cause each other pain

My windows have been shattered
Shattered beyond repair
Don't look for answers here
In the eyes of despair

These eyes once filled with love
That's been taken from me
I have shut the curtains
I'll never be able to see

Myself looking out
Or who is looking in
They will never know my story
Or where I have been

My windows have been shattered
The broken glass left me blind
My body is an empty shell
With nothing left inside

So if you were to seek the truth
Then you can go right ahead
For the state of darkness that you see
I'm as good as dead

Your Writing Space

Amarin Trichanh – Featured Poet

Poetry Prompt for 'This is Not Good-Bye'

Compose a poem that explores the deep sense of loss when someone you love passes away. Capture the emotions of grief, longing, and the void left behind by their absence. However, emphasize the idea that despite their physical departure, it is not a final farewell. Reflect on the enduring presence of their memory, the impact they've had on your life, and how their essence continues to live on in your heart and in the world around you. Use evocative language, metaphor, and poignant imagery to convey the bittersweet beauty of remembering and honoring a loved one who has passed through your poetry.

THIS IS NOT GOOD-BYE

All the pain and suffering is gone
They left and so have you
For those of us still here
We're struggling to make it through

Time is for acceptance
It does not heal the pain
We can only accept
The things we cannot change

I know you cannot move on
While your loved ones are filled with grief
But the pain of losing you
Is too devastating and deep

Worry not and rest in peace
Remember you're always loved
We will look up to the sky
While you're flying up above

You're an angel in Heaven now
We will try not to be sad
We will celebrate your life and reflect
And cherish the memories we had

Although you moved far away
You have never left my side
Or any of those you love
You're always close by

I can always feel
Your lingering essence
Whenever I'm feeling sad
It's your comforting presence

That helps remind me that
There is no need to cry

This is see you later
That this is not good-bye

So until I cross over
Make room in Heaven for me
Make room for all our loved ones
Reunited we will be

Your Writing Space

Alys Caviness-Gober

Poetry Prompt for 'Black and White Photograph'

Write a poem inspired by the contemplation of a black and white photograph depicting a father in his U.S. Navy Dress White uniform. Imagine a child gazing at the photo and asking how their mother and grandmother endured the emotional weight when he walked away, perhaps for a deployment or duty. Explore the themes of sacrifice, love, and resilience as you delve into the family's experience. Use descriptive language to convey the details of the photograph and the emotions it evokes, as well as the strength and support that bind generations together in times of separation and service.

BLACK AND WHITE PHOTOGRAPH

my father's ever-insouciant smile
the sparkle in his eyes
are clear in this blurry old photo
ready for *the adventure of a lifetime*
in crisp new Navy whites
straight out of High School
arms flung 'round mother and grandmother
their proud eyes shadowed with worry
and now I look at this photo
with children and grandchildren of my own
and I don't know how they endured

his youthful jaunty stride
in the moment he walked away

Your Writing Space

Alys Caviness-Gober

Poetry Prompt for 'Gray Wolves Circling'

Write a poem that explores the battle between inner turmoil and the soothing embrace of nature. Describe the stars as ancient sources of comfort and security, drawing a parallel between their glow and the warmth of a smile. Transition into a sudden storm, using vivid imagery to convey the intensity of nature's forces, mirroring the narrator's inner turmoil. Draw parallels between the raging storm and the emotional storm within. Conclude by highlighting the irony that, despite the narrator's efforts to battle the external storm, their words are ultimately drowned and turned against them, leaving them with a bittersweet taste of tears.

GRAY WOLVES CIRCLING

Swamped in fatigue, body and brain like glue, my head rolls
    back so I can see the only beauty left here. The wonder of
    stars still twinkle and glow like I'm still a child and they
    cover me with an ancient warmth that's like Mom's smile.
    In their silent embrace my contorted muscles relax and for
    a moment or two I'm safe. I can't even feel the tears that
    slip away from my eyes. My heartbeat slows; maybe I'll
    sleep a bit tonight.

The storm comes on in a sudden gusting of rain and wind like
    sharp knives whipping down from the fast and furious dank
    clouds that thunder in like a runaway freight train.
    Lightning flashes into snapping crackles of trees and
    branches fiercely ignited falling piercing the fragile peace
    I'd found.

My anger rises, rises, rises, like the wrath of an angel struck
    down from Heaven into Hell. Legions of gale-forces strike
    wave upon wave yet I stagger to my feet, fists raised, and

scream out my battle poem. My army of words fly with the fighting spirit of *damn the torpedoes full steam ahead* as I rage against the demon in desperate defiance.

I remember trying to hide my tears from you as we watched Gandalf shout *YOU SHALL NOT PASS*.

My words are drowned and burned and turned back onto me by the storm and I taste at last the salt of my tears.

Your Writing Space

Alys Caviness-Gober

Poetry Prompt for 'Thanksgiving Day 1950'

*Compose a poem that transports you to Thanksgiving in the year
1950, with two best friends serving in the Navy far from home in
Korea. Picture the emotional surprise as they return
unexpectedly to their families, reuniting for the holiday. Years
later, imagine the mother's enduring memory of that moment
when she can still vividly see her son coming home, bringing
unimaginable joy to the family. Use nostalgic and descriptive
language to convey the warmth, happiness, and timeless love
that defines this Thanksgiving memory, and explore the lasting
impact of such a reunion in your poetry.*

THANKSGIVING DAY 1950

I hear this story in my youth from my mother
who was eleven at the time.
The Thanksgiving meal is at always noon;
family and friends gather around
the table of Macedonian-born grandparents.
All are immigrants to America, even my mother,
who was one year old when she came here, to Portland,
      Oregon.
They are proud to be American citizens.
My grandparents' friends John and Terpana Christie are there;
Their son Ronald is far away,
somewhere off the shores of Korea.
Ronald and his best friend, Wayne, graduated high school
and enlisted in the Navy before they could be drafted.
The drafted serve without choice in the Army, with a two year
      requirement.
Because Ronald and Wayne enlisted, they must serve four
      years.
They are eighteen years old, serving on the same ship.

It is three years before the war will end in July 1953.

My mother knew, at eleven years old,
the communists are to be feared.
At school, children endure atom bomb attack drills:
> on the floor under desks
> heads covered by their arms
> teachers say this will save them
> if the communists drop an atom bomb
They tell the children: you must have food and water
and medicine in bomb shelters or in your basements
if your parents cannot afford to build bomb shelters.
The War casts a frightening shadow over America,
over this Thanksgiving Day.
At the food-laden table Ronald's father says grace:
> heads bowed, they pray for Ronald and Wayne
> and for all the brave young men fighting in Korea
> and they pray for America, their beloved country.
As he carves the turkey, they all silently echo their prayer.
Dishes are passed and soon there is the hum of conversation,
pleasure in the food and the company of friends.

The table sits a few feet from the bottom of the stairs,
where the view of the stairs, the landing, and the back door is
> clear.
Suddenly a shadow falls against the door, the door knob turns,
for a moment they feel alarm as the door opens
then on the landing appears the dazzling glow of
Ronald and Wayne in Navy whites flying down the stairs
> screams of happiness
> prayers worked
> they are here!
John and Terpana throw their arms around Ronald and Wayne
as the very air fills
with unimaginable joy.

Ronald says, "We tried to get here by noon; we did our best."
Ronald and Wayne unexpectedly were given a three-day pass:
>   one day to travel
>   one day at home
>   one day to return to the war.
Amid shouts of wonder, two place settings are added.
This precious day will last from noon to midnight
but for all who are there, it will last forever.
My mother understands this is the Thanksgiving Day
of a lifetime, the stuff of dreams.

In 1985, Mom is forty-six years old
and she's flown to Portland from Noblesville, Indiana
for her parents' 50th Wedding Anniversary party.
Among the guests are Ronald and Marilyn Christie;
after the war, they met on an airplane, married in 1957
and have two grown children, Mark and Nancy.
Ronald and Marilyn are smiling at my mother,
they move forward with open arms to greet her.

All she can see is Ronald
rushing down the stairs in his Navy whites
bringing with him
unimaginable joy.

Your Writing Space

Sarah Cope

Poetry Prompt for 'A Little Light to Light Up Your Life'

Write a poem that explores the transformative power of light in the darkness of life. Imagine how even a small glimmer of light can dispel the shadows and bring warmth to your heart and soul. Reflect on the idea that these glimmers of light, whether they are moments of hope, kindness, or beauty, have the capacity to illuminate the path forward. Use vivid imagery and metaphor to convey the contrast between darkness and light, and how these moments of brightness can offer solace, inspiration, and renewal in your poetry.

A LITTLE LIGHT TO LIGHT UP YOUR LIFE

The light of day and the darkness of night are like metaphors.
For the light in our lives, but also the darkness where upset
    occurs.
Glimpses of light are life hope through life's struggle.
Just like that little light at the end of the dark tunnel.

When pain is dragging you down into the darkness.
Those capsules of light awaken you from inertness.
They warm our hearts, reigniting our inner spark.
When the light conquers the night and drives out the dark.

It's those tenderhearted times that stop us from falling apart.
The glistening stars are balls of light that fight against the
night.
Like knights of the light their armor shimmer and glimmers
bright.
Freckles puncturing the abyss despite the blanket of the darkest
eclipse.

The light of the moon pushing through it cannot be missed of
simply dismissed.
The moon is like a big bright balloon surrounded by stars of all
shapes and sizes.
Soon on the horizon, the sun will burn through the darkness as
it slowly rises.
Dispersing the darkness of the night, just like the darkness that
plagues your life.

The sun will rise with the brightest light, and everything will
eventually be all right.
Light will always shine through even on the darkest night.
You'll see a star of two, no matter the pain or suffering you're
experiencing.
Look for those glimmers of hope.

That's the light shining down on you to warm your heart and
hands too.
That's what will pull you through the darkest times...those
glimmers of light.
Some are big, bold and brass and others mere twinkles
shooting past in the dead of night.
Finding the light in life will bring hope even in those darkest of
times.

You'll always see a glimpse of light to help you light up your
    life.
When things get tough just look up and let the lights loving
    rays bless you with a Sun kiss.
Although things might not be going right, or seem to be amiss.
For a few moments just soak up the lights luscious kiss, it's
    pure heavenly bliss.

And hey, just so you know, things will turn out all right.

Your Writing Space

Sarah Cope

Poetry Prompt for 'Life'

Compose a poem that explores the introspective moment of a woman looking at her reflection and coming to the realization that time has transformed the person she once was. Capture the sense of nostalgia, introspection, and perhaps melancholy as she gazes upon her own image and feels like a stranger with a harsh, pensive glare looking back at her. Use descriptive language, metaphor, and introspective writing to convey the complex emotions, self-discovery, and the passage of time that this introspective moment evokes in your poetry.

LIFE

She sat right there,
with a pensive glare.
She no longer saw,
herself anymore.
A reflective stranger,
stared back at her.
Lines of life,
run deep with strife.
Sunken soulless eyes,
tired from tears cried.
Lips once lushes rouge,
now anxiety chewed.
Time had taken its toll,
life had stolen her soul.
A strangers reflection sat there.
Staring back with a pensive glare.

Your Writing Space

Sarah Cope

Poetry Prompt for 'My Battlefield Cry'

Write a poem that portrays a battlefield cry for triumph in the face of temptation, where you stand alone against an enemy that seeks to take away your sobriety. This battle is not just a momentary struggle but a lifelong journey. Describe the intensity of the moment as you lift your voice and cry out against anxiety, fear, and the forces that threaten your resolve. Use powerful language, metaphor, and imagery to convey the strength, determination, and the inner war that rages on in this poetic battlefield, where victory means maintaining your sobriety in the face of adversity.

MY BATTLEFIELD CRY

I never felt so alone.
I stood on a battlefield...no Army...I stood alone.
Staring straight at the enemy in front of me.
This enemy is not stood alone.
It holds the monopoly over infantry.

It has infested and infected hundreds, if not thousands, of souls.
Yet here I stand alone.
If I must fight this on my own then I must be all powerful.
Because this enemy is strong...powerful.
The enemy often tries to entice me to join their cavalry, with
    all sorts of tricks and treachery.

It would be so much easier to join rather than standing alone.
The fight will take the willpower of all saints, even Saint
    Simon.
It will tear me apart, every piece of my being...every particle of
    my soul.
If I let down my guard for even a second, especially in the
    combat zone.

Where I will be alone...I will have lost the battle...the enemy
will have won the war.

I might as well sign over my soul to the devil as I'll be done
for.
This war will rage on for months, not weeks or days.
This is no mere feat to fight, dark days are ahead so it
forespeaks.
This enemies strength is beyond intense...I can feel its burning
glare.
It pulses sheer fear that's so tangible in the air.

As I stand here ready to fight tooth and nail, even alone for my
sobriety.
The enemy may fear me not, as they see me standing alone
against their nimiety.
But soon it will bow down to me as it loses its heavy hold and
it no longer owns.
I've never felt so alone as on the battlefield ready to fight for
freedom and redemption.
But I'd be a fool to not admit I'm not afraid.

Afraid of failure...afraid I may jump to an inference.
Afraid to become once again a captured prisoner infested with
the enemy Barbiturates.
So I stand here, yes on my own, as this fight can only be fought
by me against my enemy.
My sweet, sweet addiction.
Oh, how I wish I could just run to thee, but to do so would
surely end in my demise.

So alone I must fight, I shall charge across the battlefield, into
darkness to search for the light.
I know I can do this even if I must do it alone.
That may sound egotistical but really I'm praying for success.
I'm praying to make it, to not become another statistic.
With this war I'm about to begin and then endure.

My willpower will be tested for sure, as I fight this demon
    alone.
I pray for pure clean sobriety and freedom...a freedom from my
    addictions satiety.
I will willingly fight, with all my might, to find peace and
    harmony.
During this battle for recovery to guarantee sobriety.
To ensure a new life for me to live free from anxiety and fear.

Your Writing Space

Mary Couch

Poetry Prompt for 'Cycle of Futility'

Compose a poem that delves into the cycle of war, capturing the experience of leaving home at a young age, the harrowing struggle to stay alive amidst the chaos of conflict, and the inevitable journey of getting injured, recovering, only to realize the futility of it all. Explore the emotional toll, the loss of innocence, and the profound sense of disillusionment that comes with such a journey. Use vivid imagery, metaphor, and introspective writing to convey the enduring impact of war on those who have lived through it, and the realization that the sacrifices made may not have been worth the cost in your poetry.

CYCLE OF FUTILITY

Looking back, I was barely eighteen
when I first wore my army green.
An idealistic child headed off to war
for my mom's pride on a foreign shore.
I had felt the cause was right,
and boldly went there to fight.
Chasing evil across desert sand,
and through each village in their land.
In the midst of chaos, I could see,

those who fought were just like me
as my weapon spit death in every town,
and our bombs tore their buildings down.
I had thought this would surely be
a war to end all others fought by me.
Instead, each fraction in their land
against each other raised a hand.
Bullets flew around me in the air,
blood and death were everywhere,
and when the battle was finally done,
I realized that no one really won.
The sun shone bright on that day
the suicide bomber came our way,
as we headed forth to a local town
tracking a group of insurgents down.
He screamed to his God before he struck,
and the bomb went off against our truck.
In one brief moment I quickly found,
my body shattered on the ground.
I alone survived the bomber's death wish
as the others lay scattered about like fish.
For six months I was left to mend,
and try my best to comprehend.
Left a boy, I returned as half a man,
a dramatic change to my plan,
and in my mind, one simple truth,
gray-beard men make war, not the youth.
Bullets flew around me in the air,
blood and death were everywhere,
and when the battle was finally done,
I realized that no one really won.

Your Writing Space

Mary Couch

Poetry Prompt for 'PTSD – What's in a name?'

Write a poem that explores the complex emotions surrounding Post Traumatic Stress Disorder (PTSD). Convey the idea that PTSD is a part of the narrator's life, an ever-present companion, yet they yearn to escape its grip. Explore the duality of this relationship - how it is both a defining aspect of their experience and something they wish to leave behind. Use introspective language, symbolism, and metaphor to delve into the struggle, the desire for healing, and the hope for a life beyond the weight of PTSD in your poetry.

PTSD – WHAT'S IN A NAME?

Post-Traumatic Stress Disorder
If I could but change the name
Perhaps Please Think Something Different
Would it help to heal the trauma that haunts me?
Would it help to change the images that I see?
Can I reclaim the places stolen from me?
Will I be liberated from feelings that suffocate?
If only lye soap could scrap these ghost thoughts
embedded from the past within my mind, free me
from standing on the brink of a pool, and in the
clear water see dead and dying soldiers not serene
blue water. Remove the emotions that grab hold
of my being, and feeling once more amid the thick
of battle, not safe at home with the ones I love.
My mind continues to fight a battle to free myself
from memories, so the abusers don't win and I can
reclaim what was stolen from me.

Your Writing Space

Mary Couch

Poetry Prompt for 'Remembrance of Bobby'

Compose a poem that portrays a woman's poignant recollection of a man who was in her life briefly but went away to serve his country, never to return. Capture the fading memories of him, where all she has left are the faint smells and images in her mind. Explore the themes of loss, nostalgia, and the passage of time as she clings to these fading remnants of his presence. Use evocative language, sensory details, and metaphor to convey the bittersweet emotions and the delicate nature of memories that linger in her heart and mind in your poetry.

[Poem Inspired by Bob Dylan's Song John Brown]

REMEMBRANCE OF BOBBY

My memories of him are but the blink of a firefly.
Yet still, I feel his gentle touch, the way his arms
caressed my shoulders watching Autumn sunsets.

His midnight blue uniform reminded me of the sea,
his home away from me. The war, plays still upon my mind.
Duty for country was what he said. That foreign shore his
    destiny.

His fragrance still briefly lingers on the pillow though his
    imprint now is gone.
My letters were like books, his only notes.
The echo of his voice alone remains within my mind.

The shadows in blues brought me the news, was it just
    yesterday?
Why you I asked? No answer given.
Cold medals rest upon my mantle, a bleak exchange for love
    now lost.

His clothes are packed in boxes, sit on attic shelves.
I wait as the days slowly pass till Autumn sunsets come again.
She has his eyes of steel gray, and curls of auburn hair.

Sorrow's mantle no longer drapes me in its grasp.
I watch Autumn sunsets once again, and hold his final legacy

Your Writing Space

Bill Cushing

Poetry Prompt for 'A Decima for the Doughboys'

Compose a poem that reflects on the stark shift in destiny for young men who find themselves thrust into the horrors of war, rather than receive the joys of music and parades. Explore the contrast between the innocence and dreams of youth and the harsh, life-altering realities of conflict. Consider the sacrifices and challenges they face as they are compelled to abandon their youthful aspirations. Use vivid imagery, metaphor, and evocative language to convey the profound impact of war on these young lives and the loss of the carefree dreams that once filled their hearts.

A DECIMA FOR THE DOUGHBOYS

Influenced by the zealous praise
coming from teachers and parents
they left enthused before real sense
replaced the glow of youthful gaze,
pride, and honor with true malaise.
Troops become a sacrifice for

Mars, depleting their thirst for war.
Instead of music and parades,
a drumbeat of cannon cascades
into the trenches of world war.

Your Writing Space

Bill Cushing

Poetry Prompt for 'Drowning in Retreat in 1991'

*Write a poem that explores the somber theme of those who lost
a battle and chose to bury themselves in the sand, ultimately not
surviving. Imagine the emotional weight of their decision and
the circumstances that led to such a choice. Consider the
symbolism and reality of the sand as a burial shroud and a
reminder of the unforgiving nature of the struggle they faced.
Use powerful imagery, metaphor, and introspective language to
convey the depths of their sacrifice and the haunting legacy they
leave behind in your poetry.*

DROWNING IN RETREAT IN 1991

With the battle lost, those few who
survived buried themselves

under sand, dug in only to get
bulldozed beneath a front stretching

across 170 miles
of parched shoreline. Did these Iraqi

sons and fathers, pawns praying
to Allah, beg or shout for mercy

over the thrum of diesel engines
like surf drumming in the desert.

What god could've heard the screams
of these conscripts coming from

under those granular waves?
All noise is muffled as throats and lungs

filled with that smothering tide.
Their blood, seeping into the grains,

makes its own mud, and they—
the men never really wanting

to be there—fall victim to this,
a new and unintended assault.

(Part of '*this just in'...*, 2022 chapbook)

Your Writing Space

Bill Cushing

Poetry Prompt for 'Pictures at Five (for D.K.)'

Compose a poem that begins with the image of a boy at five years old, sitting on Santa's knee, followed by snapshots of his journey through Cub Scouts and prom. Then, transition to the present, where you contemplate that same boy now fighting for his life in a foreign land. Explore the stark contrast between the innocence and simple joys of childhood and the harsh realities of war and sacrifice. Use descriptive language and vivid imagery to convey the emotional weight of this transformation, and reflect on the profound impact of time and circumstance on a young life in your poetry.

PICTURES AT FIVE (FOR D.K.)

Kneeling on the floor,
thumbing through the albums
around me, I see
the pictures:
at five, on Santa's knee;
your first sailor's knot
in Cub Scouts;
tuxedoed for a prom. Then
you joined a different promenade,
one of brown and tattoos.
Now you bunk with
eight others in Ramadi.
Yesterday, Christmas Eve,
you called your mother and
me.

That's when I heard of the insurgent who came at you, pistol
bared,
shooting, and you,
with your M16

"not readily available,"
grabbed your knife to spare
your life. These are
not the times
I wanted for my son,
so I went back to these old shots
and remembered those days
to avoid the images I now endure
until, God willing, May.

(First appeared in *West Trade Journal* (2016); part of *A Former Live* (2019 book))

Your Writing Space

Bill Cushing

Poetry Prompt for 'Requiem for the Troops'

Write a poem that focuses on troops marching off to battle with high hopes of fame and glory, only to have their expectations shattered as they witness their fellow soldiers laid out in graves. Explore the contrast between the initial enthusiasm and the grim reality of war's toll. Describe the emotions, the sense of loss, and the haunting images that stay with them. Use powerful imagery, metaphor, and poignant language to convey the transformation from idealism to stark reality and the profound impact it has on those who experience it in your poetry.

REQUIEM FOR THE TROOPS

Marching off in search of accolades,
they left lovers, friends, and family behind
to crush those called their country's foes
and then return, exalted, after battle,

but it wasn't fame that they would find;
their pride and honor led them to be
slaughtered as their nation's cattle
or food for lice or shattered in gore.

Instead of glory, these troops had to see
limbless comrades in baskets laid in rows
in the trenches of our first modern war
hollowing out any glory in parades.

Your Writing Space

Bill Cushing

Poetry Prompt for 'Sub-IMAYO'

Compose a poem that explores the unique sensation of being submerged in a submarine deep beneath the sea. Describe the confined, submersed environment, the isolation, and the anticipation that comes with opening the hatch to the surface and breathing in the fresh air. Reflect on the profound sense of relief and gratitude that washes over you, knowing that you are alive for another day despite the challenges of the deep. Use sensory language, vivid imagery, and introspective writing to convey the juxtaposition of the submarine's depths and the life-affirming moment of emerging into the open air in your poetry.

SUB-IMAYO: USS TANG, PACIFIC THEATER

Bubbles guide us through the seas, hidden under waves:
death less than an inch away—until battle's done.
We climb ladders to clean air, and we've beaten back
enemy surface vessels—our adversaries.

Your Writing Space

Paul Gilliland

Poetry Prompt for – 'A Homage to the Dead in Flanders Fields'

Write a poem that pays homage to the fallen with red poppies in Flanders Field, a place of sacred remembrance. Picture families walking amidst the poppies, their steps measured like prayers spoken in the midst of a serene and poignant landscape. In the distance, imagine the solemn tolling of bells, their mournful chime echoing the depths of loss and gratitude. Explore the themes of memory, sacrifice, and the enduring power of honoring those who gave their lives. Use evocative language, sensory details, and a reflective tone to convey the reverence and significance of this hallowed ground in your poetry.

A HOMAGE TO THE DEAD IN FLANDERS FIELDS

In Flanders Fields, with poppies red
We pay our homage to the dead
Beneath the crosses lie the young
Across their bodies, flags are flung
As laid in their eternal bed.

These men that fell where valor led
By God appointed in his stead
At death there were no dirges sung
In Flanders Fields.

This hallowed ground where families tread
As prayers are spoken; poems are read
Throughout the year the flags are hung
And in the distance bells are rung
For here they sleep, Cross at their head
In Flanders Fields.

(First published in "Hindsights of 2020", a collection of poems by Paul
Gilliland, available at https://www.amazon.com/Hindsights-2020-
Collection-Sonnets-Rondeaus/dp/B08STHXXGT)

Your Writing Space

Paul Gilliland

Poetry Prompt for 'A Place to Take a Knee'

Write a poem that reflects on a hallowed ground where heroes rest eternally, having made sacrifices for their country in their prime. In this sacred place, distinctions of color, race, or creed vanish, and all headstones look the same, differentiated only by the names etched upon them. Explore the theme of unity in service, where the focus was on helping all souls in need, regardless of their background. Reflecting on the idea that in this place, where differences are unseen, we come together to honor and pay our respects to those who served. Use evocative language, a reflective tone, and a sense of reverence to convey the significance of this place where all are equal in their sacrifice.

A PLACE TO TAKE A KNEE

Our heroes in this hallowed ground are laid
In their eternal rest for all of time.
We honor them for sacrifices paid
Each given for our country in their prime.
We don't see different colors for the dead.
The headstones in this field all look the same.
There is no black or brown; no white or red,
The only true distinction is the name.
We do not see their race or know their creed
For this was not important to their task.
They served and helped each soul they found in need
And no request was e'er too much to ask.
Since color, race, and creed you cannot see
This is the place where we shall take a knee.

(First published in "A Heroic Crown and Other Sonnets", a collection of sonnets by Paul Gilliland, available at https://www.amazon.com/dp/1960038001)

Your Writing Space

Paul Gilliland

Poetry Prompt for 'A Soldier's Heroic Crown Sonnet'

Write a poem that reflects on the themes and messages conveyed in the "Soldier's Heroic Crown Sonnet" provided. Explore the concepts of heroism, sacrifice, unity, and the importance of seeing others as friends rather than enemies. Use these themes to inspire your own creative expression, and consider how the sonnet's structure and progression can influence your poem's form and style. In other words, make this yours while infusing it with the feeling the author poured into this work.

A SOLDIER'S HEROIC CROWN SONNET

I

As I began this tale in sonnet form
Of those heroic men of years gone by
I spoke of all the deeds they did perform
And sacrifices we could not deny
What love does man hold dear above his life
That he would dedicate himself for thee
Above his sons, his daughters, and his wife
To thus ensure that future men live free
These brave young men who volunteer to serve
Who give their life for such a greater good
For liberty they die so to preserve
A constitution rarely understood
For why one lays his life down for a friend
It's often hard for some to comprehend

II

It's often hard for some to comprehend
For plots are often twisted with surprise
But knowing of a life lost by a friend
The actions of his life I must reprise
Though with some women he had learned of love
Or more perhaps the pleasure found in sex
Commitment was not what he sought thereof
Not falling under any woman's hex
For he was satisfied to share his life
In service for the betterment of man
And thus had no desire for a wife
For that was never in his lifelong plan
But as his life had started to reform
I saw the message of his tale transform

III

I saw the message of his tale transform
As I began to see deep in his soul
For in his mind there stirred a constant storm
Of which he seemed to have no known control
As governments declare that countries are
A detriment to life as we now know
It's in the eyes of soldiers that are there
Who shan't see foreign citizens as foe
For people all throughout the world have needs
To live their life in peace and harmony
And we should never blame them for the deeds
Of evil ones in the minority
To make things right I hereby recommend
To understand the life of my dear friend

IV

To understand the life of my dear friend
I had to see the truth that he revealed
For he had said "right" often did depend
On things that in the open were concealed
He told me once that battles are not fought
By those who make decisions for a war
But rather by the ones who have been taught
That there is more than they are fighting for
For it is just the young they send to fight
That suffers from the trauma he endures
While politicians watch to their delight
The public's loud opinion reassures
To make your choice this story will unfold
This tale of one heroic man of old

V

This tale of one heroic man of old
Has long been kept in secret thus is said
But now the time has come that it be told
In hopes that through the land his tale will spread
A young man with wild dreams and high ideals
Set off to join the army in his prime
For honor, glory, liberty appeals
To those who see a mountain there to climb
At first, they're smitten by romantic dreams
Of grandeur as they face a faceless foe
But battles aren't romantic, so it seems
When bullets end the lives of those you know
But honor will not make the tears decrease
When giving all to bring forth worldly peace

VI

When giving all to bring forth worldly peace
He saw the frightened faces of the foe
And no sane way to conjure the release
Of conflict that his heart had come to know
And so, throughout the years this struggle grew
Beginning to infest his conscious thought
'Til it was hard to see which facts were true
And if these wars were simply all for naught
But yet he held on to his firm belief
That leaders had an unseen master plan
For in the end, it would relieve his grief
By warranting the righteousness of man
But after years the truth would thus unfold
As stories long forgotten were retold

VII

As stories long forgotten were retold
In hopes that man would learn from days gone by
But yet it seems those stories where controlled
And what was told was often just a lie
They say the victor writes the history book
And thus, their point of view is kept alive
However, it may mean that we've mistook
For fact the written fiction they contrive
With truth erased the masquerade goes on
True faces hidden underneath the masks
As future generations thereupon
Are asked to undertake aforesaid tasks
The spinning carousel of life must cease
To see the violence all around decrease

VIII

To see the violence all around decrease
We must treat every neighbor as a friend
For only love can give us the release
To open up and truly comprehend
Our inner soul does best when it's at peace
A long life comes from laughing and from smiles
For only when all wars and battles cease
Can man appreciate the different styles
Perhaps the cost of conflict is the bane
That keeps the global finances in black
Large armies now each country must maintain
Ensuring that no others will attack
For hidden in the darkness of the night
The enemies know not those whom they fight

IX

The enemies know not those whom they fight
There is no face of which to recognize
Attacking from the shadows out of sight
Relying on the aspect of surprise
For meeting opposition face to face
Can add a human factor to the game
By showing some compassion in this case
May indicate that we are all the same
For what about each other do we hate
Does innocence mean anything in war
This moral question's subject for debate
An answer each man's conscience must explore
For we would choose between what's right and wrong
If every person could just get along

X

If every person could just get along
The world would be a better place indeed
So, when in history did it go wrong
Was it because of power or for greed
Did people fear those different than them
Were they afraid of how their lives might change
And so, those that they feared they would condemn
Convincing all the others they were strange
They caused division all throughout the land
With neighbor hating neighbor for a lie
As rulers forced each one to take a stand
It's very few that ever asked the "Why"
And as they added fuel to the fight
Within each quest there is a path to light

XI

Within each quest there is a path to light
That opens up the soul to all things true
We all are made aware of this despite
The trials that each man must first pass through
For we must learn to show ourselves respect
And love oneself above all other things
Alone this has an altering effect
With clarity that to our being brings
This sense of peacefulness within our heart
A calming aura that engulfs our soul
The knowledge that the ancients do impart
Are qualities that make our spirits whole
They guide us down a path that can be long
Where thoughts of every person can belong

XII

Where thoughts of every person can belong
Opinions of all people can be heard
Together there is one voice loud and strong
When open-mindedness is what's preferred
But when the voice of some is drowned out
By those who still refuse to compromise
Attempting to be heard they start to shout
And dark misunderstandings start to rise
If only everyone would realize
That in the end we all have the same goal
To live in harmony is for the wise
When every part contributes to the whole
We find that compromise will not offend
If we can see each other as a friend

XIII

If we can see each other as a friend
The conflict in your life will be reduced
Although your way of thinking you defend
Ideas new to you are introduced
You always need to keep an open mind
Another's thoughts have merit as do yours
And if the thoughts of both can be combined
It may not lead us to so many wars
Whenever you are in a foreign place
Beware of wolves that wear a lamb's disguise
The truth is shown within a person's face
The window to the soul is in their eyes
For if we treat each stranger as a friend
We now can bring this cycle to an end

XIV

We now can bring this cycle to an end
I'll tell you now of how my hero died
It was not in the ways that Fates intend
But rather in a way that he'd decide
You see, his mind was full of lasting grief
Of horrors he had seen because of war
For orders contradicted his beliefs
But yet there was no way he could ignore
As he looked in the other people's eyes
He took and put the gun up to his head
His conscience led him to his own demise
As he then took his own flawed life instead
For he had seen the enemy transform
As I began this tale in sonnet form

XV

As I began this tale in sonnet form
It's often hard for some to comprehend
I saw the message of his tale transform
To understand the life of my dear friend
This tale of one heroic man of old
When giving all to bring forth worldly peace
As stories long forgotten were retold
To see the violence all around decrease
The enemies know not those whom they fight
If every person could just get along
Within each quest there is a path to light
Where thoughts of every person can belong
If we can see each other as a friend
We now can bring this cycle to an end

(First published in "A Heroic Crown and Other Sonnets", a collection of sonnets by Paul Gilliland, available at https://www.amazon.com/dp/1960038001)

Your Writing Space

Paul Gilliland

Poetry Prompt for 'To Veterans'

Write a poem that pays tribute to the sacrifices and dedication of Veterans who spend their youth in distant lands, away from home, defending their country's call. Explore the themes of duty, loyalty, honor, and the selflessness of those who choose to serve in the military. Reflect on the idea that these heroes willingly sacrifice themselves for the greater good, embodying greatness within their ranks. Convey the profound gratitude and respect we hold for Veterans, and emphasize that their sacrifices will always be remembered and honored. Use these themes to inspire your own poetic expression and capture the essence of appreciation for those who have served.

TO VETERANS

They spend their youth in far off distance lands
And holidays are spent away from home.
They make a bed 'neath dunes of drifting sands
Or underneath a bombed-out palace dome.
A duty to defend the country's call
With loyalty unto their brotherhood
In honor proudly standing straight and tall
To sacrifice themselves for greater good.
This life is what these heroes chose to serve
For greatness is among the ranks of these.
The highest praise is what these few deserve
For life to them is but a day to seize.
And so, we give our thanks to every Vet
For sacrifices we will not forget.

(First published in "Hindsights of 2020", a collection of poems by Paul Gilliland, available at https://www.amazon.com/Hindsights-2020-Collection-Sonnets-Rondeaus/dp/B08STHXXGT)

Your Writing Space

Paul Gilliland

Poetry Prompt for 'We Shan't Forget'

Write a poem that reflects on the deep gratitude and remembrance for the sacrifices made by those who answered their country's call. Explore the themes of duty, honor, and the commitment to defending freedom above all else. Consider the different ways in which these heroes may have been cut down or lost their lives, whether in battle, through accidents, or other means. Focus on the enduring significance of white crosses and the names engraved upon them as symbols of remembrance. Emphasize the importance of displaying flags as a tribute to these heroes. Use these themes to inspire your own poetic tribute to those who have given their all, and the vow to never forget their sacrifice.

WE SHAN'T FORGET

We shan't forget the price they paid
And noble sacrifices made
By answering their country's call
Defending freedom over all
Until Taps final note was played

If cut down by the horseman's blade,
The shrapnel from a stray grenade,
Or enemy's lead rifle ball
We shan't forget

Upon the fields where men are laid
White crosses form a colonnade
With names engraved so we recall
The heroes who each gave their all
With each and every flag displayed
We shan't forget

(First published in "The Poppy: A Symbol of Remembrance", an Anthology from Southern Arizona Press, available at https://www.amazon.com/dp/B0BFR2N2WP)

Your Writing Space

Derrick Iozzio and Kim Gwinner

Poetry Prompt for 'Blessed'

Write a poem that explores the ups and downs of life, acknowledging that there will be messy days but also moments of blessing and love. Emphasize the importance of reaching out to peers and finding support during difficult times. Highlight the idea that sharing our struggles with others can lead to healing and personal growth. Encourage the idea that writing can be a therapeutic outlet for expressing thoughts and emotions. Ultimately, convey the message of hope, resilience, and the power of connection in navigating life's challenges and finding strength in the journey.

BLESSED

There are days in life you're going to feel like a mess.
But every day you get to live, you'll be blessed.
By the little things you might not see or do.
Please know that you are loved, if even by a few.

Yes, there will be days when you feel messy.
On that, you can count, but don't let it stress thee.
For you have survived those days, more than a few.
Surrounded by others who really love you.
Keep going and do what you do.
Spread the love to others from me and you.

On our messy days we can still be strong.
Your guide can help you and you won't be alone.
The journey we take can feel so long.
Peers supports are here for you like a chaperone.
We want to help you to stay on your course.
But only when you are ready to do the work.
If you need information, we can find a source.
Who knows you might end up writing a book.

I have had those days; I was a mess.
Those days I tried.
Those days I lied.
To a peer, I was able to confess.
That peer knew I couldn't hide.
Like dust on a shelf.
I was only fooling myself.
A peer is someone who has been there.
A person with a story to share.
A peer knows how to care.
When you find yourself in a mess.
Find a person and talk out the stress.
Soon you will feel better.
And maybe even write a letter.
Explain how you took a look.
Inside yourself.
And like my friend, write a book.

I too, have had messy days.
In fact, most of my life was in such an array.
I cried.
I tried to say goodbye.
To a peer I was able to open up.
And release all of that messy stuff.
And after doing so, I felt much relief.
That in myself I began to believe.
That there were people in which I could trust.
Because on this healing journey that is a must.
Not only that, I found I could trust myself.
And was able to remove that dust from my shelf.
I found the people to talk out my stress.
And now my days are less a mess.
Thank you for being here when I do need help.
Because I know that you care, and it is heartfelt.
On paper we should keep writing our words.
To keep our progress from going backwards.
We don't want to go back to the past, what a mess.

Remember that each day we live we are blessed.

Your Writing Space

Kim Gwinner

Poetry Prompt for 'Allowing Others to Love Us'

Write a poem that explores the idea of allowing others to love us as a reward for fighting our internal battles. Reflect on the process of opening up and allowing ourselves to be vulnerable, even if it feels unsettling or challenging. Emphasize the courage it takes to dismantle the protective walls we've built around ourselves. Consider the gradual nature of this process and the idea that it's okay to take small steps towards letting others in. Highlight the potential for growth, healing, and connection that comes from accepting love and affection from lovers, friends, and others. Encourage readers to embrace the journey of self-discovery and allowing love into their lives when they are ready.

ALLOWING OTHERS TO LOVE US

Allowing others to love us.
That is the reward for fighting our battles.
Even though we may have to adjust.
It may even make us feel a little rattled.

Allow it to happen just the same.
And let our hearts be repaired.
Because that is a wonderful thing.
Even though we may feel impaired.

Removing the bricks from our wall.
Is true bravery and that's no lie.
Even though we may feel small.
Go ahead and give it a try.

The wall will not come down all at once.
So, there will still be that protection.
And it may feel like a ball bouncing.
But allow from others to feel their affection.

From a lover, a friend, or someone else we may know.
We have to let them in from time to time.
That is the only way that we will grow.
Whenever you're ready to try that is fine.

Your Writing Space

Kim Gwinner

Poetry Prompt for 'I'm Thankful for that Every Day'

Write a poem that celebrates personal growth and healing. Explore the transformation from a state of brokenness to a place of healing and gratitude. Describe the shift in mindset from anger and turbulence to a more positive and peaceful outlook on life. Highlight the importance of self-care and the positive impact it has had on well-being. Emphasize the appreciation for small joys and the ability to enjoy music and simple pleasures. Convey the message that despite occasional challenges, each day is an opportunity for growth and living life to the fullest, and express gratitude for the progress made.

I'M THANKFUL FOR THAT EVERY DAY

I was broken but now I'm healing.
I'm no longer bouncing off the walls and ceiling.
My mind is slower than it once was.
Which is much healthier because.
I no long am angry or full of rage.
I'm thankful for that every day.

When I wake up it's with a positive thought.
Even though when I sleep battles are fought.
I don't wake up in the middle of the night.
And that in itself is dynamite.
And if I must say.
I'm thankful for that every day.

Don't get me wrong I still have episodes.
Yes, I'm not yet completely mellowed.
But I don't ponder about my past as long.
And I'll play a happy - feel good song.
Because music is something that I crave.
I'm thankful for that every day.

I spend time taking care of me.
That's my daily good deed.
For I am learning how important self-care is.
And there's no test or a quiz.
But it's healthy anyway.
I'm thankful for that every day.

As long as my emotions are equal.
Then I'll look forward to the sequel
And to live my life to the fullest.
I can even have my own funfest.
A single event or an array.
I'm thankful for that every day.

Your Writing Space

Kim Gwinner

Poetry Prompt for 'I May be Broken but I am Repairable'

Write a poem that explores the journey from a place of trauma and isolation to one of understanding and planning for the future. Describe the transformation from a life that felt bleak to one filled with hope, social connections, and the creation of new memories. Emphasize the courage and determination it takes to welcome these changes and step outside of one's comfort zone. Capture the essence of embracing life, having fun, and pursuing joy. Convey the message that no matter how challenging the journey may be, the desire for healing and the pursuit of a fulfilling life are worth the effort.

I MAY BE BROKEN BUT I AM REPAIRABLE

From trauma central to understanding.
I have a future in which I am planning.

A social life I am forging - I shall no longer isolate.
New and fresh memories - a life I will create.

Learning to have joy and some fun.
I'll be ridding my trike for I can't run

If you see me at the park or on a trail.
Just know that I haven't failed.

I have to welcome these changes I seek.
To get out of my world that been so bleak.

I'm sure it will be tough at first.
But I have this hunger and massive thirst.

I no longer want to be broken.
Yes. those are words I have just spoken.

Because I know I am repairable.
For wasting my life is so damn terrible.

Your Writing Space

Kim Gwinner

Poetry Prompt for 'Space'

Write a poem that explores the need for personal space and reflection. Describe the importance of taking time to collect one's thoughts and find a quiet place for self-discovery and healing. Emphasize that this need for space doesn't necessarily mean isolation; it can be a shared experience with someone supportive. Reflect on the therapeutic aspects of activities like listening to music, writing, or simply finding a peaceful moment before bed. Convey the idea that creating space for oneself is a valuable part of the healing journey and a way to find clarity and peace of mind.

SPACE

Sometimes I just need space.
Time to collect a thought or two.
I can probably do it anyplace.
Anywhere on my healing avenue.

Sometimes I just need space.
But not necessarily alone.
We can even do it at your place.
To clean off my bloodstone.

Sometimes I just need space.
To listen to my music loud.
And this need not be a race.
But where it will be allowed.

Sometimes I just need space.
To write a poem about my past.
But not to be on a preplanned pace.
And not for too long let it last.

Sometimes I just need space.
To clear my head.
Just to give my thoughts some space.
Especially right before going to bed.

Your Writing Space

Chris Hasara

Poetry Prompt for 'Hook and Loop'

Write a poem that delves into the metaphorical concept of pain as Velcro on our skin, a relentless force that clings to every rough-edged memory and keeps us bound to the past. Explore the idea that pain makes it impossible to look away, to numb ourselves, or to escape its grasp. Convey the intensity and persistence of this emotional pain, which refuses to let us go until it becomes the only semblance of peace we can imagine. Encourage a deep exploration of the emotional and psychological impact of pain, and how it shapes our perception and response to the world around us.

HOOK AND LOOP

Pain puts Velcro on our skin,
double-sided bristles that
grab every rough edged
memory they brush against,
grinding it into our
ever crying eyes,

Refusing to let us look away.
Refusing to let us not feel.
Refusing to let us.

Until only
the flaying knife
looks like peace.

Your Writing Space

Chris Hasara

Poetry Prompt for 'LT'

Write a poem that explores the complex emotions of a person who was not physically present in a warzone or combat situation, but who carries the weight of the experience and loss endured by those who were there. Delve into the sense of survivor's guilt and the haunting presence of the memories and sacrifices of others. Describe how the echoes of the past continue to reverberate, even for those who were not on the front lines. Capture the bittersweet blend of distance and presence in the narrator's relationship with the events of the desert and the lasting impact on their life.

LT

I wasn't there
in the desert.

I had a young bride
and wider plans.
Like him,
like all of them.

So I was home,
and not in the convoy.
I played pool in dark bars.
Someone played taps.

I wasn't there.
I am there always,
long after they
carried him home.

Your Writing Space

Chris Hasara

Poetry Prompt for 'Tied in Ribbons'

*Write a poem that explores the bittersweet return of friends
who have come back from a war or conflict. Delve into the
complex emotions and changes that occur when people return
home after experiencing the trauma of war. Describe the mix of
familiarity and strangeness in their faces and smiles, and the
sense of disconnection or inner turmoil that lingers beneath the
surface. Explore the idea that while they physically came back
home, a part of them may remain elsewhere, forever changed
by their experiences. Capture the nuanced emotions and the
challenge of reintegrating into civilian life after witnessing the
harsh realities of conflict.*

TIED IN RIBBONS

They all came home,
my friends who fought
for the right to choose
to stay or to go.

Every face familiar,
every smile strange,
like new clothes on
old store mannequins.

And in every eye that
would meet mine, I saw that
they all came home
but didn't
come home
all.

Your Writing Space

Chris Hasara

Poetry Prompt for 'Up Early Morning'

Write a poem that explores the deep, almost mystical connection between a soldier and the earth or land they have fought on. Describe the calling or beckoning of the land, especially when it holds the remains or memories of conflict. Explore the idea of transformation, where the soldier is shaped and molded like clay into a warrior, a protector, and a servant of a higher purpose. Delve into the dichotomy of being both a soldier and a human, and how this dual identity can be both empowering and challenging. Capture the sense of duty, sacrifice, and transformation that comes with the role of a soldier, especially in the context of war and battle.

UP EARLY MORNING

I hear Her calling
from the red clay,
foundations where I push
myself up and up and up.

Calling to me,
begging me, cajoling me,
commanding me to be all,
the fullest self, stretching every
limit of my skin.

Queen of Battle.
She knighted me,
kissed me on the forehead,
sent me on my way.
To focus, to train, to serve.

Mighty infantry,
baby's made soldiers,
men made sacrifice,
clay fired
into useful
discardable shapes.

Your Writing Space

Lon Hodge

Poetry Prompt for 'Cathedral'

Write a poem that captures the poignant and complex relationship between memory, nature, and the experience of hunting. Describe the scene of a deer near red rock spires, its antlers and the buckskin grass in the Colorado sun, highlighting the vivid imagery of the environment. Explore the memories of a past hunt, where the father struggled with health issues, and the narrator, as a witness to it all, felt a mix of emotions. Convey the idea of a deep and unsettling connection between hunting, life, death, and love. Consider how the act of hunting can both connect and distance people from nature, and how memories of such moments can be both haunting and cathartic.

CATHEDRAL

Below open spires of red rock
A deer rinses dead skin
From his shriveled antlers
Then hobbles away
Browsing buckskin grass,
Color gone worthless
In the relentless Colorado sun.

He has turned broadside to me,
But he is safe.
I have no weapons but memory.

Our last hunt here,
My father had to stop
Every few feet
To beg for air.

I went ahead
And prayed for a miracle
That I flushed from the low cedars.
And ran straight toward my father,
Who pulled the trigger
Without time to aim.

It is a horrifying love
That commends a toothless man,
Who is kneeling before a bloody animal,
Laughing, gasping, laughing.

Your Writing Space

Lon Hodge

Poetry Prompt for 'Corpusant'

Write a poem that explores a moment of profound and unsettling natural beauty, with vivid descriptions of the landscape and wildlife. Describe the hawk soaring through the twilight, the breeze rustling the grass, and the trees etching their presence against a darkening sky. Convey the senses of awe and violence in the scene as the hawk captures the rabbit, and the trout leap in the pond. Use powerful imagery to depict the storm gathering, with ground lightning and the heartbeats of mortars echoing through the night. Explore the juxtaposition of the natural world and human world, as the narrator reads a letter amid the chaos of nature and seeks refuge in their car. Capture intensity of the moment, with elements of danger, beauty, and contemplation.

CORPUSANT

From an outflung wrist of rock
I watched a hawk glide toward dusk
One wing wrapped around an orphan wind
The other steering him through the receding light.

A night breeze began scavenging
The tremoring grass
Trees began to scrimshaw faces on the darkening sky.

A rush of feathers above me
And then I saw the rabbit
His ears, laid back, talons pierced his ribs.
He never flinched and easily resigned
As some frightened animals do.

Cutthroat trout in a nearby shallow pond
Leapt into the enormity of night.
Ground lightning, corposant.
Began coursing between the boulders.

My heart slammed like the mortars
Falling through the night
I read your letter as it thundered without rain

Night-blinded by the flash and rumble
My hands reached for the hot breath of the road below.
I was cut stumbling through the knives
Wielded by dew drenched cottonwoods
Before falling against the glass and steel
Of my empty car covered in the shivering sweat
Of a thousand cold stars.

Your Writing Space

Lon Hodge

Poetry Prompt for 'From the Shore'

Write a poem that delves into the complex relationship between a father and son, tied together by the shared experience of fishing. Begin with a serene scene by the lake, with the moon overhead and the father's lures calling the son to action. Describe the father's presence, with his distinctive scent and the tangible memory of him. Explore the passage of time, with the son reflecting on his own life choices and how he's come to accept his father's wisdom and heritage. Convey the son's deep emotional connection to his father, especially as he reflects on the night of his father's death, promising to take him fishing again. Explore the idea of the lake as a symbol for the father's influence and legacy, and how the son continues to seek connection and meaning through the act of fishing and memories of his father.

FROM THE SHORE

Over the lake's granite surface
The moon's blind eye kept watch
As small as golden stars fell. Lures cast
By my father would raise my sleepy head.
I would listen for fish to wound the calm, flare
Into the enormous night air, and fight him
Reeling them toward shore. One night
In my late teens, An indecisive breeze touched us
I remember the familiar odor of age, cigar ashes
Rubbed into overalls, and Lucky Tiger hair balm
On a black forever military scalp.
At thirty-five or so, I quit my ascensions away
From his tobacco farmer beginnings:
I accepted I was no match for the strength of experience,
The tattooed arms and yielded to his eighth-grade smugness
And the once embarrassing southern vowels: long lines

That could coax fishing tackle to scribble success
Across a lake. I walked its circumference the night he died
And listened to icy respirations give in to winter.
Drowning in his own fluid, he sometimes smiled
A delirious toothless smile, like he'd just landed a keeper.
I promised, no lied to him. I would take him Fishing again.
Then his eyes went white: turned inside, toward the water,
His naked fingers queried the deep, dry pocket of his head
    wound.
It was a year after the seizure his arms fell limp at his sides
And the man who could not read anything but inland tides
And solunar tables lay helpless in a hard bed.
They say it was pneumonia. I say it was the lake
Claiming him. I returned his ashes: reticent,
Swirling near the bank they ebbed toward the center
Where I still cast lure after lure
Fishing for the moon.

Your Writing Space

Lon Hodge

Poetry Prompt for 'The Last Bear Hunt'

Write a poem that captures the tension and anticipation of a hunter's encounter with a majestic and ominous creature, perhaps an eagle or a vulture, drawn to a grisly scene of scavenging animals. Set the scene with vivid descriptions of the gruesome aftermath, where squirrels and other animals are feasting on remains in the harsh sunlight. Explore the arrival of the majestic bird of prey, described as 'Huge and noiseless as dusk,' and convey the eerie stillness that envelops the moment. Build suspense as the hunter takes aim with the arrow, describing the delicate balance between heartbeats and the bow sight's movement. Convey the hunter's internal struggle and the final decision to release the arrow, capturing the profound connection between predator and prey, life and death.

THE LAST BEAR HUNT

I am spending the last of my patience
Watching squirrels
Chase over maggots and fish heads
And bones steaming in the sun.

Sunset is beating a tambourine of light
Through the trees. He is coming,
Huge and noiseless as dusk.

He is here to feed
On the already dead,

He hovers,
A black cloud
Over the stench
Then paws the pile into a boil.

I draw back the arrow.
My bow sight,
Held over his chest,
Leaps and hesitates
In time with my heart

I let go of the arrow
So slowly
We both hold our breath.

Your Writing Space

Lon Hodge

Poetry Prompt for 'Wenchuan'

Write a poem that captures the resilience of a community in the aftermath of a devastating event, such as the Sichuan earthquake. Describe the scene of a once-ruined countryside now showing signs of life, with weeds and flowers pushing through the rubble. Convey the sense of renewal and hope brought by spring, contrasting it with the haunting memories of the past. Illustrate the daily routines and connections among the survivors as they come together for activities like morning tea and mahjong. Explore the unspoken bond among them as they check each other's hands for trembling when construction trucks pass by, symbolizing their shared trauma and the strength they find in one another.

WENCHUAN

Through the scattered rubble
Of Sichuan's broken countryside
Weeds and flowers grow again.

It's Spring and birds scream
While we meet for morning tea and mahjong

We draw straws for seats closest to the door
We will never play for money again.

Children we barely know pass by
Always walking in the middle of the road
Far from the new glass-filled windows.

When the construction trucks roll by
And our glasses shake
We quietly check the other's hands for trembling
Then run our own through thin and graying hair

It's the only way we speak of it these days.

Your Writing Space

Derrick Iozzio

Poetry Prompt for 'I am One of the 22'

Write a poem that conveys the heartfelt message and plea of a U.S. Military Veteran who represents the '22,' referring to the tragically high number of Veterans who take their own lives every day. The poem should capture the essence of the veteran's message, emphasizing the importance of reaching out for help and supporting fellow Veterans who may be struggling with the invisible wounds of war. Explore themes of camaraderie, brotherhood/sisterhood, love, sacrifice, and the idea that there is hope and help available. Use the veteran's voice to inspire others to take action and be a lifeline for those in need.

I AM ONE OF THE 22

I am one of the 22. I am a U.S. Military Veteran, and I am speaking for my brothers and sisters who are the 22. I am calling out to you from under the U.S. flag. We took the same oath as you. We swore to defend our country. Like you, we did this with honor. We experienced things that no human should have to experience, but we did because we were Soldiers, Marines, Air

Force, Navy, and Coast Guard. We answered our country's call to serve.

We completed our service, we tried to return home, to our families, our loved ones, our lives. Many of us were able to do just that, but not the 22. We became lost, we could not reach what we once knew. We were not able to find the direction, nor the help. This we bore as a heavy burden and we could no longer bear this burden. Our cries for help were unspoken at times, and at other times, it was our behaviors that did the talking but went unnoticed. We could not see any other way, so we gave in, we just wanted to end the pain, the suffering and we did the only thing we could at the time.

We never meant to cause anyone the pain, the heartache, the sadness that they now feel. We now know that the path we took was not the correct way. We cannot change this, but we can help others find the right path. We have much love for all of you, but we no longer have a voice to tell you. We can no longer express our love with actions, words, or deeds, but our love is there, and it is eternal.

As one of the 22, I am asking on behalf of myself and my brothers and sisters that you who are living, you that are able to speak on our behalf, to use your voice, your actions to tell others that which we cannot tell. Hear me as I speak from under this flag.

My message is simple but urgent. Do not join our ranks, we love you and we admire you brothers and sisters but do not join us in the way that we have. Look to your brothers and sisters, your loved ones, reach out, and ask for help. There is no shame in asking for help. When we all wore the uniform, we helped each other. Nothing has changed.

Will you be our voice? Will you be our eyes? Will you be our ears? Speak on our behalf, look for our brothers and sisters, listen to them. Watch them, talk with them, hear them. Help them find their way, do not let them join our ranks. There is hope, there is help.

We can no longer speak for ourselves; we need your voice. Help us to help our brothers and sisters. Spread the word, take action, help us to stop our ranks from growing. We served together in the past, and we can serve together now, our memories and your actions will save lives. Get involved, find that local Veteran organization in your area of operations, reach out to them, and ask how you can help. Find that fellow Veteran who is struggling, help them find their way. Together we can do much good.

I am one of the 22, calling out to you from under this flag, hear me, family.

Your Writing Space

Larry Murley

Poetry Prompt for 'Bring Flowers to my Grave'

Write a poem that pays tribute to the courage and sacrifice of individuals who served in various wars throughout history, from the Civil War to the modern conflicts in the Middle East. Use the refrain 'Bring fresh flowers, sweet Mary, here to my grave, Bring flowers, sweet Mary, I died trying to be brave.' to emphasize the common thread of bravery and sacrifice that runs through their stories. Explore the changing nature of warfare, from the Civil War to the technological challenges faced by soldiers in recent conflicts. Conclude with a reflection on the importance of finding alternative solutions to conflicts and preserving the lives of the young generations.

BRING FLOWERS TO MY GRAVE

Bring fresh flowers, sweet Mary, here to my grave,
Bring flowers, sweet Mary, I died trying to be brave.

It was in the summer of 1862, that I first went to war,
Down south to Dixie, to give them Rebs what for.
As he fell wounded, he died being brave,
He said to me brother, I never owned a slave.

Bring fresh flowers, sweet Mary, here to my grave,

Bring flowers, sweet Mary, I died trying to be brave.

Then again when the 20th century
Was still in its infancy
I went afar with the infantry
I fell in Flanders Field, in muddy mess
Why, was anyone's guess

Bring fresh flowers, sweet Mary, here to my grave,
Bring flowers, sweet Mary, I died trying to be brave.

Then in 42, I left our small farm,
On Normandy's beach, I faced great harm,
My buddies all charged that great beach,
But it's Sandy soil I didn't quite reach.
As the water ran red with all our gore,
We washed upon that hallowed shore.

Bring fresh flowers, sweet Mary, here to my grave,
Bring flowers, sweet Mary, I died trying to be brave.

Korea was our next killing field
But to Communism we could not yield,
So when the drums played and the bugles would sound,
We stood strong; we held our ground.
And when charge was over, and we counted our dead
My body was counted, my mother's one dread.

Bring fresh flowers, sweet Mary, here to my grave,
Bring flowers, sweet Mary, I died trying to be brave.

In Viet Nam, in the jungle so hot,
Midst smells of powder, and bodily rot,
We fought for our buddies, we tried to stay alive
The VC came in the night, like bees to a hive.
At Ia Drang, and Da Nang, and Pleiku
We wrote our letters and thought of you.

And when we were ready to rotate home,
Sometimes we only came home to a Garden of Stone.

Bring fresh flowers, sweet Mary, here to my grave,
Bring flowers, sweet Mary, I died trying to be brave.

Then came Desert Storm, and a desperate attack,
In 2001, we got shot in the back,
And we all headed for the desert sand
To fight again, to the very last man.
War had taken a technical turn,
But it didn't stop the bullets burn.
We still have not left that battlefield,
Our foe has decided that they won't yield.
So maybe it's time to rethink why we go to fight,
Maybe it's time to save our young knights,
To not send them to a sandy grave,
But to find leaders who think outside the box,
And when politicians rise up, give them the pox.
Let them go to an early grave.
And keep our young people, we know they are brave.
They can fight hunger, and disease and more,
And save our planet, and preserve our shore.
We need young minds, and strength of drive
To help us find answers to help us survive.
As we of past generations, go visit the grave ,
Of past generations, who proved they were brave.

Bring fresh flowers, sweet Mary, here to my grave,
Bring flowers, sweet Mary, I died trying to be brave.

Your Writing Space

Larry Murley

Poetry Prompt for 'The Captive'

Write a poem that captures the harrowing journey and resilience of an individual who escapes captivity and navigates through a perilous jungle to find freedom. Explore themes of determination, survival, the power of the human spirit, and the triumph over adversity. Describe the physical and emotional challenges faced during this journey, as well as the profound sense of strength and wisdom gained from such a life-altering experience. The poem should convey a message of hope, resilience, and the indomitable will to survive against all odds.

THE CAPTIVE

The jungle at night under a growing moon,
I halt in step, for fear of man, and not too soon.
I escaped a fate far worse than death,
Slipped into that jungle, in a hare's breath.
From a small cage made from Green Bamboo,
To a walk in a jungle full of dangers through.
The moon give light to a narrow trail,
'neath the high trees, the heavens are frail.
No North Star I can find, to point the way,
So then I need to travel by day.
God knows, I cannot follow that plan,
Else I will not live through this land.
I am lost, in no man's land, deadly beasts are about,
I must pick and choose, a correct route.
Or else I die, and no one will ever know,
"What happened to him, where did he go."
I walk all night, my heart in my hand,
What kind of food is found in this land.
Well, none I will find for all this day to eat,
Tomorrow I may perish on my own two feet.
"Those two feet", you stop and say,

"they will not last you another day".
Torn and bleeding, from thorn and stone,
Each step extracts a silent moan.
The bottom of each foot, ragged and sore,
Beg you, "Hey Boss, please, not one step more.
But no, I will not stop, nor will I die,
Even though days ago, I wanted to try.
Yes, I reached the end, I wanted to die.
Please, No more, I wanted to cry.
I didn't though, nope, I'm mad.
Things are where it could get bad.
But, I will not let you inside me,
And somehow, some way, I will be free.
When you try to steal a man's will,
You take him as close as ever to a kill.
You do it over and over again,
It drives you a while to a point of insane.
But caution yourself, at that low space.
You are playing God, it's not your place.
You can break a body, you can cause pain,
Just remember inside that body, is a live brain.
If that brain is able to escape and flee,
It will turn that body in its fury against thee.
But you know all that, and maybe a bit more,
Laying on your bed, covered in Gore.
But thanks anyway, my strength is reborn.
These tiny hardships, this pain, I scorn.
And days and weeks did crawl by,
Under a hot Wet Asian sky.
And that long trail did finally end,
And home was just around that bend.
Sometimes at night, I take that walk.
Where growls and shrieks and monkeys talk.
Where a smell or a sound in the night,
Halts your steps, breath grows tight.
Then in caution you go on toward your goal,
These lessons, give wisdom to your own soul.

I want to ask, as nice as I can,
Have you ever known fear, understand?
I mean fear, that you must hold check,
Or else, you cannot expect to save your neck.
To be alone, in a strange land
A hundred miles from a friendly hand,
Alone in fierce place, men looking for you,
And the jungle itself can just as easily eat you.

And you know, if I survived all that,
Life will never ever throw off my hat.
I can do it, whatever it may be,
Nothing will ever match that you see.
So my word of wisdom, lend me your ear.
Blessings are sometimes disguised, hidden by fear.
So if life threatens more than you can bear,
Remember maybe someone else has been there.
And regardless how bad it might be.
You can conquer it all, the strength is in thee.

Your Writing Space

Larry Murley

Poetry Prompt for 'Garden of Stones'

Write a poem that pays tribute to the resilience and sacrifices of Veterans throughout American history. Explore the experiences of a veteran who has served in various wars and reflects on the changing landscape of the nation, both in terms of external conflicts and internal challenges. Touch on themes of duty, loyalty, the impact of war on individuals and society, and the enduring hope for unity and progress in the face of adversity. The poem should convey a message of respect, gratitude, and the ongoing commitment to preserve the principles upon which the nation was founded.

GARDEN OF STONES

As I walked among the stones that morn,
A shape ahead of me began to form.
A Soldier from days gone past,
Behind him flags flew at half-mast.
I hurried my step, to join his side.
There was little need to lengthen my stride.
A much-lined face, with short grey hair,
He chose his path with determined care.
His dress was a puzzle to say what war
Had taken his youth, had shaped his core.

I asked him, "Sir, where did you serve?"
He answered, "Wherever America thought best deserved.
My first battle was on our eastern shore
To separate us from oppression evermore.
Then before the cannon had ceased its fire,
I fought again, in different attire.
And before our country was a century old,
We fought again, a tear, in our nation's fold.
With flesh and blood, we healed that tear

And swore nevermore to allow ourselves there."

I looked at the medals upon his chest.
There Purple and Bronze and Silver did rest.
He saw my gaze and followed my eye.
"It was in Flanders Field; I did almost die."
His finger traced to the next bright star.
"Thirty years later, on Normandy, so far.
This was from Korea, in the cold and ice.
This in Viet Nam, in paddies of rice."

His gaze dropped on his brow in a crease,
"Then, next we were called to the Middle East.
We went, and fought, and gave it our best,
But what we want is to give war a rest,
To go home and work and go to school,
Not to shed our blood for some greedy fool.
Don't mind me, Sir, if I appear sad,
But war was the only life I had.
I gave to my country all that was asked.
I never shirked from duty or task.
But, Sir, (a tear rolled down his cheek),
"Why have our people grown so weak?
Our leaders, instead of choosing for us
Security and support, throw us under the bus.
While we were away, serving their need,
Our leaders seem drunk with power and greed.
They fight over points that have no bearing
For a country with a record worthy of sharing.

They want to ban from our nation's berth
Peoples from all over God's Green Earth.
Most excuses they choose offer no reason.
To restrict our growth comes close to treason.
How can we continue to be a city on a hill
When new blood we need is steadily killed.

And our citizens, it is worth to note,
Choose to give up their blessing, the right to vote,
And go merrily along with mind in 'coast,' frivolity and
ignorance they dwell on most.
Aw, Sir, I don't mean to complain.
If asked, I would serve just the same.
But, somehow, it doesn't seem fair
That half of our people seem not to care.
some of the other half are simply not there.

What great event could make us united
Remains yet secret, not yet sighted.
But, Sir, don't fret.
We will lick this thing yet.
Just remember, we gave our all to be free.
Soldiers of the past, for you and for me.
And some of us will not stand by
To let America sicken and die.
We stand our duty, to tell all of our home
And walk though eternity in this garden of stones."

Your Writing Space

Larry Murley

Poetry Prompt for 'Mama's Love'

Write a poem that captures the poignant moment of receiving news about the loss of a loved one, particularly in a war context. Explore the emotions of the family as they gather together to celebrate a birthday, only to be met with the heartbreaking news of a son's death in Vietnam. Describe the contrast between the joyful family gathering and the sudden arrival of two uniformed officers delivering the news. Convey the deep sorrow, grief, and the enduring love for the lost son, Danny. Explore themes of sacrifice, loss, and the resilience of family bonds in the face of tragedy.

MAMA'S LOVE

The rain was pouring down visibility was blind,
late in a Illinois evening, June 7th, 1969.
We had gathered at home, in this land of sweet earth,
It was mama's celebrating her 60th year since birth.
Around the Piano we gather our selves
Her grandchildren were scampering like little elves.
We sang Happy Birthday, to that sweet soul,
Her years of labor and devotion showed all the toll.
Her face show lines of worry, sometimes a tear.
There was one absent, one she held dear.
You see Danny boy, he was serving Uncle Sam,
Danny, the baby had gone to Viet Nam.
A year he had been gone, short 30 days.
But still every morning she arises and kneels and prays.
You see Danny, had been sickly from the very start,
Her labors with him, made it harder to part.
Just this morning, a letter had come,
"Mama, tomorrow, I am flying out from Kon Tum.
Our company, is rotating you see,
Our next stop won't be so dangerous for me.

We will go to Da Nang, and play on the beach,
And last day here will soon be within reach"
Mama's hands shook as she read that short note,
She sat down with hands folded, wiping tears on her coat.
We smiled at each other, and witnessed her love,
Her eyes looked up, not at us, but above.
We drank a toast to her and Dan,
Mama, fear not you raised a fine man.
Then wind blew hard, we could feel the house rock,
And then at that moment, there came a knock.
Bill, the eldest, he walked to the door,
When opened the rain blew in on the floor.
Outside two men in Uniform stood,
Erect and silent like statues of wood.
Bill bade them enter and closed the door,
They stood for a moment dripping on the floor.
"Mrs. Brown, the oldest one said,
I regret to inform you; your son Danny is dead.
He was killed in action, just last night,
In what would have been his last flight.
Mama' legs folded and she sank to the chair,
She would have fallen to the floor if son Sam was not there.
From back in her throat, came a low cry,
And tears started falling from both her eyes.
Oh Danny, Oh Danny, Why did you go,
You knew that I loved you, I loved you so.
She lay sobbing at all our feet,
The Officers took this time to retreat.
We knelt all around her, so she could feel love,
And yes, we could feel Danny standing above.
We told her that too, and it seemed to console.
It was then that Mama started to grow old
And Mama only lived for ten years more,
and she would hardly ever look at that door.
It reminded her of her loved one so dear
Mama loved her family, and kept us near,
Then came another dark rainy night

she called us to her, with eyes so bright
And when she gathered us around her bed,
she smiled, I love you all, and, Danny's not dead.

(written 9/10/2018)

Your Writing Space

Larry Murley

Poetry Prompt for 'PTSD'

Write a poem that explores the journey of healing from deep emotional wounds and trauma. Consider the metaphor of healing emotional scars in the same way physical wounds are treated. Express the idea that healing is a process that takes time and understanding, and that confronting and addressing past traumas is essential for growth and recovery. Use imagery and symbolism to convey the transformation from darkness to light, from fear to strength, and from being controlled by past experiences to taking control of one's own destiny.

PTSD

You say to me, I wish to heal,
I say to you, how do you feel?
You say my scar lies really deep,
I ask why is it there, that you it keep.
You say the demon is dark, I hide it inside,
Then it is you, who allow it to abide.
Demons are creatures of the dark,
You duty is to make them fear and depart.
You must let light into your mind,
And seek out wisdom of the sublime.
A wound to flesh, you will need to treat.
Is a wound to the mind, no less challenge to meet.
A slash from a knife, you bandage for a time,
Then open the wound to air and sunshine.
Our hearts and minds are healed in the same way.
But healing comes not in a single day.
Such expectations will disappoint all who expect,
We must understand the malady and give it respect.
It is a product that was born of ancient man,
To keep him from danger in a lawless land.
He would experience great fear,

And then later, would not allow it to come near.
But time has gone by and we have seemed to evolve,
and our lessons should be less traumatic and easier to resolve.
If we have to experience a terrible event,
understand it is a lesson for eternity not meant.
So find down deep in your heart's mind
a reason that what happened needs not to bind.
And allow not that picture to come to your dreams, day or
    night,
and continue not to cause you sorry and fright.
Know that they were an event in your life,
And not meant to continue your strife.
Bring forward and tell their whole story,
Allow them not to have their dark glory.
You are unique and are master of your mind,
a result of thousands of years, of a progressive mankind.
Take strength in yourself, you are the boss.
Tighten up the cinch and take the bit now, hoss,
and ride into the sunset, down a dusty trail.
And fear not, you wear a white hat, you will prevail.

(written 6/29/2023)

Your Writing Space

Gloria Nesloney

Poetry Prompt for 'I Hide Inside'

*Write a poem that explores the idea of finding solace and peace
in a personal inner realm, separate from the external world's
worries and troubles. Describe the experience of escaping from
the chaos of everyday life into a place of tranquility and
connection with the divine. Use vivid imagery to convey the
sense of leaving behind the noise and commotion to enter a
sacred, hidden sanctuary where one can find solace, clarity, and
the presence of a higher power. Reflect on the contrast between
the external world's challenges and the inner spiritual refuge.*

I HIDE INSIDE

I seek a realm of peace,
I lay my weary head.
I drift between time and space,
I am free here instead.

My spirit soars and takes flight,
higher than high.
Nothing is concealed
in the midst of my eyes.

Contours, shapes, colors, flavors, smells, emotions.
My spirit is part of all the commotion.
I am above, below, in the middle, or seeing from afar.
All these scenes I see, it's really bizarre.

Who can know the dreams I've dreamed?
Or the visions I have seen?
Who can tell when I was awake to see the drama.
Or if I was one who knew these and escaped the trauma.

The days had been filled with worries, troubles, and cares.
A list cannot fit all of the enemies flares.
When the time has come to ignore the shame and pain
I embrace that place inside of me no one can take away.

The terrible truth of it all is that no one can know
The places I've been, The places I walk, or the places I go.
I capture my thoughts, the casualties of those that scream.
I toss them behind like leaving them into the sea.

Then with millions around or when I am alone
I quiet my spirit to enter into a place it belongs
I slip past my body and soul for just a little while
And I hide inside with my LORD and wait for HIS smile.

(First published online on June 24, 2021 at
https://www.lightforeverynation.com/post/i-hide-inside)

Your Writing Space

Gloria Nesloney

Poetry Prompt for 'It Hurts'

Write a poem that serves as a heartfelt tribute to a beloved sister and friend who has passed away. Express the pain and sadness of losing someone dear, while also celebrating the person's life, character, and the positive impact they had on others. Reflect on the strength, courage, and faithfulness of the departed, highlighting the cherished memories and moments shared together. Emphasize the belief that even in the midst of grief, the presence of the Lord provides comfort and solace. Explore bittersweet emotions of loss and gratitude, acknowledging that while it hurts to say goodbye, the departed loved one has left behind a legacy of love and cherished memories.

IT HURTS

It hurts...to say thank you Lord...
for giving me a great Sister and Friend.
You saw that she is faithful and true
So you wanted her closer to You.

My Sister, you ran well.

Yes, it hurts...but Lord you know what is best.
Now my friend can truly find rest.

To those who know you, you will be missed,
Family, friends, and the angels you have kissed.

When It still Hurts, Lord, you have given us all an example of
Strength, courage, and gentleness...
Sarcastic, punny, and silliness.

When going through the toughest trials anyone could endure,
Her foundation in You was sure.

The joys we shared,
The times when we were scared,
The clock just ticked on, we didn't care.

Now the hands of time have stopped today for you my Dear.
Sister Friend, I know you and Jesus will be drying our tears.

Well done good and faithful is hard to say
because It Hurts to know we don't have another day.

(First published online on June 24, 2021 at
https://www.lightforeverynation.com/post/it-hurts)

Your Writing Space

Gloria Nesloney

Poetry Prompt for 'I Know There's One'

Write a poem that explores the transformative power of faith and the love of Christ. Describe a person's journey from a place of despair, heartache, and hopelessness to a newfound sense of hope, purpose, and renewal through their encounter with the love of Christ. Highlight the idea that, no matter how broken or lost someone may feel, there is always a source of unconditional love and acceptance waiting to embrace them. Convey the message of faith, redemption, and the belief that, in the midst of life's challenges, there is a love that never ceases and a path to healing and salvation.

I KNOW THERE'S ONE

There had been a pounding in my heart,
My world was crumbling, falling apart.
But one day that changed my life
It's when I heard about the Love of Christ.

Tell me, who could ever want me
after all that I've been through,
Who would want to love me,
I'm sure there is one, let it be you.

At first I said there is no hope.
Where could I turn I'm at the end of my rope.
Then Jesus said to me, "My Child come to me.
I will give you rest and set you free."

Tell me, who could ever want me
after all that I've been through,
Who would want to love me,
I guess there is one, I hope it's you.

So I closed my eyes,
lifted my hands and
answered to the call.
Lord, I cried, take my life I give you my all.

He has given me a reason
To live life today,
Cause His Love never ceases
And forever His love will stay.

Tell me, who could ever want me
after all that I've been through,
Who would want to love me,
I know there is one, it's only you.

(First published online on June 24, 2021 at
https://www.lightforeverynation.com/post/i-know-there-s-one)

Your Writing Space

Courtenay M. Nold – Co-Contributor/1st Editor

Poetry Prompt for 'Battle Cross'

Compose a poem that delves into the emotional turmoil of a survivor experiencing the weight of survivor's guilt. Describe the internal struggle of someone who has witnessed loss and trauma, and now grapples with the haunting presence of those who did not survive. Emphasize the sense of responsibility and the need to find a purpose or path forward in the face of these memories. Convey the tension between the desire to honor and remember the fallen and the emotional toll it takes on the survivor. Explore the idea of closure and healing while acknowledging the ghosts of the past that continue to influence the survivor's life.

BATTLE CROSS

I closed my eyes so I could see.
The challenge right in front of me.
My head, it aches.
My limbs are sore.
A search for comfort forevermore.
My brain and heart ceased their conversation.
As I overthought, my heart was breaking.
Survivors guilt is all I see.
They're standing right in front of me.
I've found my path to walk upon.

I'll follow them until they're gone.
Gone from mind and from my heart.
My breath, it quickens as I absorb the sight.
The Battle Crosses lined up by three.
I close my eyes but then I see.
The ghosts stand firm in front of me.

Your Writing Space

Courtenay Nold

Poetry Prompt for 'Darkness and Light'

Compose a poem that explores the theme of duality, the interplay between light and darkness, and the complexity of the human experience. Highlight the idea that our perception and understanding of the world can shift like the eyes adjusting to different lighting conditions. Use vivid imagery to convey the struggle with inner demons and external challenges, and how they sometimes overlap. Consider the concept of balance and how it can be disrupted, leading to feelings of isolation and loneliness. Ultimately, reflect on the idea that beauty and discovery can be found even in the most unlikely places, and that navigating the contrasting forces of life is part of our journey.

DARKNESS AND LIGHT

eyes adjust to darkness
just as they do to light
demons approaching claw by claw
into the darkened crevices

                       Ghoulish dancing in your head

playing with fear...sadness...the unknown
hiding behind a glassy gaze
nurses who don't believe you're ill
cackles reverberate from their lair

           while they hover over their drug-laced cauldron.

whilst in a chilled chamber you try to sleep
anger burns the senses but we hide our fiery eyes
trust taking a prolonged vacation
from the cage built in our brains

There is no balance by opposing forces

of light and dark sustained
at night...at night...
our silent cry of loneliness
puzzled bodies taken apart and left to lay unassembled

but there is still beauty in darkness.

if only we knew to see
if you wish to change the stars
dancing upon a moonlit passage
you have to search the darkest paths

Within your world you are escaping

within your shape and time
seeking light in haggard darkness
and dark in fertile light
to discover the harmonic duet between

impossibility inside the mind.

Dark or light...Yin or Yang

Your Writing Space

Courtenay Nold

Poetry Prompt for 'The Forgotten One'

Compose a poem that delves into the profound theme of trust, its fragility, and the consequences of trust being broken. Explore the emotional turmoil and isolation experienced by someone who trusted others but felt abandoned in a time of need. Reflect on the impact of trauma and the battles fought within one's mind. Use vivid imagery to convey the sense of being left behind and the struggle to regain a sense of self and purpose. Highlight the complex emotions of anxiety, panic, and the erosion of self-esteem. Convey the feeling of being discarded and forgotten by those who were supposed to offer support and mentorship. Ultimately, explore the enduring strength and resilience that can emerge from such challenges.

THE FORGOTTEN ONE

why is trust so easy to break
a career thrown away when help was needed
when 9-liners invaded my dreams at night
what little I slept, my brain did fight
to escape, I pulled myself along
the headaches had already gone on too long
my trust in others...they turned their backs
hiding behind their Hesco walls
I lowered my guard and reached out for help
a battle in mind, body and soul
my anxiety, my panic, was out of control
I couldn't trust doctors, manipulation reigned
behind the screen of acted games
I found that I was just a simple pawn
given up and then I'm gone
no one
no one
stayed in touch

my mentors stranded me in stagnant rust
my ego stained; my life upturned
with nowhere to go...nowhere to run
just detailed as the forgotten one

Your Writing Space

Courtenay Nold

Poetry Prompt for 'Fortified Walls'

Write a poem that explores the essence of poetry as a means to uncover and express one's emotional core. Delve into the sensation of emotions moving slowly, like the sluggish pace of a snail, within the self. Use vivid imagery to convey the idea of words sprayed onto the page like graffiti, each word carrying the weight and intensity of the emotions within. Explore the transformative power of poetry as it deepens the emotional experience, akin to the color crimson, and how it finds its place on the canvas of a crumbling page. Consider the act of poetic expression as a form of breaking down barriers and fortified walls that may hinder authentic emotional communication.

FORTIFIED WALLS

Poetry is my search for an emotional core
Internal blood creeping along at the pace of a snail
The only way to communicate through fortified walls
Spraying words out like artist graffiti
Deepening crimson
Alighting upon a crumbling page

(previously published online by Poetry Society of Indiana at
https://www.facebook.com/PoetrySocietyIN)

Your Writing Space

Courtenay Nold

Poetry Prompt for 'Imagined Angels'

Compose a poem that delves into the interplay between light and darkness, and the emotional and existential journey it represents. Explore the idea that life is a solitary path to be explored, where one must confront both the illuminated and shadowy aspects of existence. Use vivid imagery to depict the contrast between light and darkness, such as a candle illuminating unexpected facets of life and the fear of the unknown lurking in the night. Convey the struggle of individuals as they grapple with their own inner demons and seek understanding in the midst of darkness. Consider the role of imagination and the idea that "imagined Angels" may not always guide, leaving individuals to navigate the complexities of life on their own. Explore the transformation and growth that can occur when one confronts and embraces both light and darkness, finding a harmonious balance between the two. Ultimately, the poem should convey a sense of hope and resilience, as individuals search for light and warmth amid the shadows, and angels of hope guide them towards a brighter future.

IMAGINED ANGELS

Imagined Angels never guide you
Life is a simple path to explore alone
Lighting a candle illustrates life
In unexpected ways
Like a child to bed...full of dread
Tiptoeing to trick a monster
Propelled by fear and the nightlight in the hall

In enveloping darkness
Searches begin within
Steps light on cobblestones

Escaping is impossible
If the darkest paths
Are left unsearched
Wings of dust adrift in wavering light

Slender fingers upon waves reaching
For well-worn woven comfort
Awaiting its time
Hung 'pon spindled rocker
Imagined Angels cannot guide you
Life isn't a path to explore in flight
An ignited glow illustrates life

In unexpected ways
A flashlight creates shadows
Each being in tow shaking off their countenance
By turning out the light
Desiring the trade of dark and light
Struggling until they accept shadowy forms
And own their shape in time

Seeking light in haggard darkness
And darkness in fertile light
Discovering a harmonic duet
Between darkness and light
Consciousness grows unheeded
Creating epiphanies in the mind
Searches develop senses of echoes on empty streets

Timid footsteps escaping into impossibility
If the darkest paths are left unsearched
When reappearing...who would we be
Particles of light in darkness
Souls imprisoned are floating
On purgatory and pain
Unable to reach your heaven

Repairing to middle ground
Wayward lights afloat in silence
Steps in darkened nothingness
Dusty wings adrift in wavering light
Slender fingers tracing patterns upon the sand
Longing for an absent shore
And a well-worn blanket there

Hung 'pon a spindled frame
The sails, they sigh, with weathered breath
Above...overflowing stars
The path in flight exploring
Mind's persuasive but opposing forces
Echo's envelop the wandering lost
Carried by troubled souls

Angels of hope still navigate darkness
Finally lifting a soul to warmth

Your Writing Space

Teresa Pruitt

Poetry Prompt for '37.2'

Compose a poem that explores the profound impact of loss and heartache on a person's physical and emotional well-being. Begin with the scientific fact that the human body consists of an average of 37.2 trillion cells, highlighting the vastness of the body's complexity. Use this as a metaphor to describe the feeling of emptiness and sorrow when a loved one departs. Convey the idea that each of these 37.2 trillion cells represents a moment or a memory connected to the departed person, and that their absence is felt on a cellular level.

Explore the emotional journey of grief and the way it permeates every aspect of one's being, causing a "jolt of anguish" that reverberates throughout the body. Describe the physical and emotional toll of this loss, emphasizing the depth of sorrow experienced "37.2 trillion times."

Ultimately, the poem should convey the profound nature of grief and how it can affect every aspect of a person's existence, from the scientific to the deeply emotional, as they grapple with the absence of a loved one.

37.2

37.2 trillion average cells
in the human body.
When you left......
I felt a jolt of anguish....
.......37.2 trillion times

Your Writing Space

Teresa Pruitt

Poetry Prompt for 'Let Me In'

Write a poem that explores the theme of empathy and understanding in the face of someone else's suffering. Describe the frustration of the person who is witnessing the suffering, as they want to help but don't fully comprehend the depth of the pain and trauma the other person is enduring.

Highlight the importance of coming together and fostering a connection to end the misery and provide support to the person in distress.

LET ME IN

I've not been there,
I don't understand.
But I do care,
so take my hand.
Take me with you,
through your bad dream.
Allow me to
see what you've seen.

Dreams can be
worse than the real.
Let me see
to help you heal.
Alone one stands
but two together
hand in hand
can conquer better.

So let me in.
Enlighten me.
Let's put an end
to your misery.

Shed some tears,
ease your pain,
erase your fears,
and your life regain.

Your Writing Space

Teresa Pruitt

Poetry Prompt for 'The Blanket'

Compose a poem that delves into the concept of pain as a shared but uniquely personal experience. Emphasize that pain is a universal human emotion. Use vivid imagery and metaphors to convey the diverse ways in which people experience pain. Highlight the idea that pain can manifest in physical, emotional, and psychological forms, making it a complex and multifaceted sensation. Conclude the poem by emphasizing the importance of empathy, listening, and being there for one another in times of pain, even if we can't completely understand or articulate each other's experiences.

THE BLANKET

How can I write about your pain?
I also have pain that I carry.
It's not the same as your pain.
We use the word pain like a blanket.
Like this one small word, pain, can cover all varieties.
We throw the word around like a pillow
letting it fall the same on everyone.
There are as many different pains
as there are stars in the sky.
External pains, scrapes, bruises, broken bones,
needles, surgeries, childbirth.
I gave birth, others gave birth
but my rendition of birth pain
is different from others.
Some plead for the epidural
But I chose a natural birth.
Both had different outlooks on the pain.
Others wanted help to not feel pain
while I wanted to feel it and relive it.
People go to the dentist,

they know the pain that awaits them
but they require no laughing gas.
When I go, I desire the gas, pills, and all I can get to not feel.
Again, our perception and anticipation of pain
affects our fears, our choices and our reactions.
We see someone's outside appearance
after a major car wreck or sickness.
Our souls moan and groan in agony just looking at them.
Our compassion flows because we relate
their physical wounds to our life experiences
of cuts, bruises, and broken bones.
Seeing their condition makes us believe
that we could never endure their shoes.
But the worst pain....
the worst pain we all experience,
.......Is the pain no one sees,
a pain that fills up the inside of you.
Constantly flowing from
a vast dark hole within
and leaving you tormented inside.

No one sees it,
understands it,
or feels it,
and some even reject its reality.
You feel that you are left completely
.........Alone.......
.......just you and your inner pain.
You know not how to cope.
The pain has taken over to the point
that you've given in and given up.
You believe that you cannot endure this condition,
a condition that is killing you from the inside out.
Times you burst into a rage to try to relieve it.
Other times you go fetal, hoping
if you stay asleep and don't move
the pain will go find a new place to dwell.

But it hangs on and makes your life hell.
If the relief for your pain,
could just be found in a pill or a drink,
you would religiously consume it all to kill it.
If the answer could be found in a book,
you would read from sun up to sun down.
If the answer could be found in another human,
you'd hunt them down to get the answer.
But, pain,......
well inner pain plays its own game,
with its own rules.
Sometimes it is like "hide and seek",
It's gone and then you find it.
Sometimes it like a game of "chase",
you are running and it's right on your heels,
ready to tag you.
Other times, pain plays a "poker game",
and you are dealt a losing hand.
In most any game in life,
the more you play,
the more you comprehend,
the better you become.
But the internal pain is playing for the gold.
It will fight to the end to win.
It thrives on you giving up.
Pain can only win if you are defeated.
So, we gotta strive to obtain understanding.
See, we did not create our own hearts.
Our hearts were formed to feel love.
That is why pain hurts us.
We are able to compare the good, painless,
feelings of inner peace and love
to the torture pain produces.
Pain tries to rob us of our peace.
It's pain's way of playing.
Pain's rules: to kill, steal and destroy.
But it is far from a game to us in life.

It is a life altering experience.
Although pain is at times devastating,
we must seize the opportunity
to overcome the pain and create
a new level of understanding within ourselves.
We can beat pain at its game!
I can only try to understand and overcome my own pain,
the pain that I have experienced.
I can use the experience from my pain
to help console others
who share my similar pain pattern.
We all have pain,
but each blanket has a different pattern.
I have pain
but it's not the same as yours.
So how can I write about your pain?

Your Writing Space

Kate VerSluis

Poetry Prompt for 'Being Alone'

Create a poem that explores the paradox of being alone but not feeling lonely, highlighting the sense of contentment and inner peace in solitude. Use metaphors and imagery to convey the idea that, in the stillness of solitude, one can find solace and connect with their inner thoughts and emotions. Describe the beauty and serenity that can be found in the absence of external distractions. Conclude the poem by celebrating the paradox of being alone yet not lonely, underscoring the value of finding peace and fulfillment within oneself, even in the absence of company.

BEING ALONE

Being alone is ok. When I'm alone I worry not of what others may think. I can sing the most sorrow of songs without the looks or the question of what's going on.

Being alone is ok. I can scream at the top of my lungs and not worry that I scared another.

Being alone is ok. I can sit in the dark and cry with no one to touch me or try.

Being alone is ok. I don't have to pretend. There is no forced smile. I don't have to be happy so someone else isn't sad.

Being alone is ok. For alone, I do not have to fear the dreaded touch. I do not have to pretend that a hug is welcome and ok.

Being alone is ok. For being alone I don't have to lay next to someone and pray they don't want to touch. I don't have to worry that my movement or my mood will wake them.

Being alone is ok. Being alone is the only place I can truly be me.

For others think they know me yet they only see the shell.

They cannot see the blackness in my head.

They cannot see the turning of my soul.

They cannot see the panic with every breath.

To others I am a vision of someone who has it all. To others I have no reason for the anxiety, the fear, or the sheer desperation.

You see being alone is ok. Being alone is the one place where I don't want to kill myself because I can express who I am and not fear the judgment.

Being alone is ok.

For without being alone, I could not be.

Your Writing Space

Kate VerSluis

Poetry Prompt for 'I Want to Love You'

Compose a poem that delves into the theme of wanting desperately to both give and receive love yet feeling uncertain and inexperienced in matters of the heart. Reflect on the internal struggle and vulnerability that come with not knowing how to give or receive love effectively. Highlight the fear of making mistakes, hurting others, or being hurt in return. Explore the idea of learning and growing in matters of the heart, acknowledging that love is a journey of discovery. Emphasize the importance of patience, self-acceptance, and taking small steps toward understanding and expressing love.

I WANT TO LOVE YOU

I want to love
Yet I don't know how
I am so broken inside
So frozen in fear

Stolen from me my very being
Discarded with the power
Left to weep
Left to die
What is left to give
Oh, for all I do is cry

I want to hold your hand
Yet I don't know how
I try to reach
I am so broken inside
Frozen with each tear

Stolen from me my very being
Discarded with the power
Left to weep
Left to die
What is left to give
Oh, for all I do is cry

I want to feel your touch
Yet I don't know how
My reflexes cringe
I am so broken inside

Stolen from me my very being
Discarded with the power
Left to weep
Left to die
What is left to give
Oh, for all I do is cry

I try to tell you
But I cannot speak
I try to tell you
But all I do is weep

Stolen from me my very being
Discarded with the power
Left to weep
Left to die
What is left to give
Oh, for all I do is cry

I want to lay beside you
Warm within your touch
Yet my body cringes

Stolen from me my very being
Discarded with the power
Left to weep
Left to die
What is left to give
Oh, for all I do is cry

Your Writing Space

Kate VerSluis

Poetry Prompt for 'The Darkness Screams'

Compose a poem that explores the concept of darkness as a living entity that resists the approach of light. Explore the tension between darkness and light, highlighting how the darkness reacts and resists when someone attempts to reach out to the light. Describe the struggle and conflict between the two forces. Conclude the poem by offering insights or lessons about the nature of darkness, the persistence of light, and the potential for transformation and growth even in the face of resistance.

THE DARKNESS SCREAMS

I know I need to
Yet the darkness screams

Yes, it will help
Yet the darkness screams

I want to
Yet the darkness screams

I get to the door
Yet the darkness screams

I almost say it
Yet the darkness screams

You reach out to me
Yet the darkness screams

I almost take your hand
Yet the darkness screams

I push you away
As the darkness screams

I close my eyes and relive it all

And the darkness screams

And the darkness screams

Your Writing Space

Marilyn Wolf

Poetry Prompt for 'Courage'

Compose a poem that delves into the dual nature of a person: one side that instinctively flees from fear, and another side that courageously stands still in the face of adversity. Explore the tension and conflict between these two sides, illustrating moments of decision and choice when the person must decide whether to run or stand their ground. Delve into the emotions, thoughts, and inner struggles that accompany these decisions. Consider what it means to confront fear and adversity, and whether one side ultimately prevails over the other or if there is a delicate balance between the two.

COURAGE

Courage is the ability to keep your feet from moving when the rest of you is running away.
— Unknown

Your Writing Space

Marilyn Wolf

Poetry Prompt for 'I Sat With the Broken'

Compose a poem that explores the theme of hidden brokenness in people's lives. Think about revealing the hidden brokenness that exists within everyone. Use vivid imagery and metaphors to convey the idea that everyone carries some form of inner pain or emotional scars, even when it's not apparent to the outside world. Explore the idea that understanding, and empathy can arise when we acknowledge the brokenness in ourselves and others.

I SAT WITH THE BROKEN

I sat with the broken
it was me
I didn't know it
at the time

I sat with the broken
it was you
I knew it but you didn't
at the time

I sat with the broken
it was them
we saw it
at the time

I sit with the broken
we learn to fix each other
when necessary
at the time

(previously published online on Poetry Warrior via Facebook at
https://www.facebook.com/groups/945323226710286)

Your Writing Space

Marilyn Wolf

Poetry Prompt for 'My Champions'

Create a poem that celebrates the resilience and courage of those who serve in the military. Illustrate the sacrifices they make, both personally and on behalf of their country. Reflect on how their actions embody the spirit of champions and inspire others to recognize the value of sacrifice and service to a greater cause and communicate those thoughts in what you write.

MY CHAMPIONS

Man
Femme
Mine is
Family
Military is
Family service
They are champions in my life

(previously published online at Medium.com http://medium.com/ February 19, 2021)

Your Writing Space

Marilyn Wolf

Poetry Prompt for 'The Wound Nearly Killed Me'

*Compose a poem that delves into the theme of invisible scars
and the profound impact of individuals who offer support and
assistance during moments of extreme vulnerability. Start by
describing the wounds, both physical and emotional, that you've
endured. Transition to the pivotal role played by those who came
to your aid when you needed it the most. Explore the idea of
resilience and the strength that can be found in human
connections.*

THE WOUND NEARLY KILLED ME

the wound nearly killed me
permanent damage
my face scarred beyond recognition
bleeding out the life I had before
loss on a scale I couldn't comprehend

found the right people
to help scoop me off the floor
put me back together
their patches my patches
permanent holes left open

you'll never see my scars
but they almost killed me

(previously published online on Poetry Warrior via Facebook at
https://www.facebook.com/groups/945323226710286)

Your Writing Space

Contributor Biographies

Amarin Trichanh – Featured Poet, born Thephy Amarin Vorachak November 16, 1975 is an immigrant from Thailand. Amarin migrated to the US on August 17, 1984 with her parents and two older siblings through the refugee program to San Diego, California. Having endured physical and mental hardship during the two years of confinement in the Thai refugee camp, Amarin witnessed murder, violence, and rape at a very young age. In order to show gratitude for her new found freedom and better life, Amarin enlisted and honorably served in the U.S Army as a logistic specialist and combat medic healthcare specialist from April 10, 2002 to January 13, 2015 with three combat tours in Iraq (OIF IV 2004-2006 and OIF VII 2007-2009, and Operations New Dawn 2010-2011). She was honorably discharged from the Army on January 13, 2015. She is a published author and you can access her books here: *I Am My Sister's Keeper*, https://www.amazon.com/Am-My-Sisters-Keeper-Confessions/dp/B08FNV2MVK; and *From the Bottom of My Heart*, https://www.amazon.com/Bottom-My-Heart-Amarin /dp/B09CGHRX8T

Alys Caviness-Gober is a disabled anthropologist, artist, and writer. She taught Anthropology, Women's Studies, and ESOL at the university level, and was a PhD candidate in Applied Linguistics until her disabilities worsened in 2009. In 2011, she began selling artwork (*Creative Expressions Arts*), and soon after was juried into the *Hamilton County Artists' Association* in both their photography and 2D categories. Alys and author Sarah E. Morin are the cofounders of the literature-based annual project *Noblesville Interdisciplinary Creativity Expo* (NICE). In November 2014, she founded *Logan Street Sanctuary, Inc.* (LSS), an all-volunteer 501(c)(3) Arts organization and the organization took over hosting the annual *Noblesville Interdisciplinary Creativity Expo* (NICE) project and in 2016 took over publishing the annual anthology *The Polk Street*

Review. In July 2019, LSS rebranded as *Community • Education • Arts* (CEArts). She is a FY2017 (July 2016 - June 2017) Indiana Arts Commission *Individual Artist Project* Grant Award recipient, for which she created a series of large-scale paintings expressing life with hidden disabilities. Alys was selected to participate in the IUPUI Arts and Humanities Institute's *Religion Spirituality, and the Arts* 2018/19 Seminar Class, and has been an invited presenter at *Poetry Society of Indiana* conferences since 2017. She is a selected poet for *INverse: Indiana's Poetry Archive*, and a member of both *Noble Poets* and the *Poetry Society of Indiana*. Alys' poetry has been featured in global anthologies since the 1980s, in the *Last Stanza Poetry Journal, The Polk Street Review*, and in her own poetry and artwork collections, *Naked In Wonderland (Volumes I, II, III, IV)*. She has served on the Noblesville Cultural Arts Council and is active in the local arts scene. Alys' artwork, photographs, and poetry have received national and international recognition. Visit https://creativeexpressionsarts.com/store/c3/Books.html to view her books.

Sarah Cope/#iwriteitall is a novice writer of Child and Adult fiction, and a published poet. Writing became her Savior, after surviving a domestic violence relationship, then being diagnosed with a chronic illness, dyslexia, and then ADHD. Luckily, she's had a great support network who convinced Sarah to continue to write.

Mary A. Couch is not a Veteran, but her Brother Arthur D. Couch served in the U.S. Army, and her cousin Martin G. Hawkins was a U.S. Navy Midshipman, cousin Mark Couch served in the U.S. Navy flying helicopters and instructing others on flying. Also, the poem about Bobby was written after she received a letter back from a boy she was writing to in Vietnam, his name was Bobby Sloan and he was marked MiA. She is an Administrative Assistant for Taylored Systems LLC, a technology company in Noblesville, Indiana. She learned the art of poetry from her mother and two grandmothers who were storytellers and artists. She and her late mother, Alice Couch, published a chapbook of their poetry titled *Two Views.* Mary enjoys writing poems showing her Celtic heritage by revealing the spirits that live in nature and the oneness of the universe. Her poems have been published in a variety of venues including *Poetic Nature in the Hoosierland, Twin Muses: Art & Poetry, An Evening with the Writing Muse, The Polk Street Review, Encore, Pegasus,* and *Poetry and Paint.* She is published on Amazon with five books: *Hoosier Haiku: Poetic Snippets from the Heartland, Hoosier WordArt: Communing with the Chippewa, A Garden of Thought Blossoms, Hoosier WordArt: Finicky Kitten's Book of Rhymes, Hoosier WordArt: Generations,* and has two new books coming in 2023: *Nibby Ankleman, Dog Detective and Other Poems,* and *Mischief's Book of Scary Poems.* Mary is a past Premier Poet for Poetry Society of Indiana. You can view Mary's poetry on https://www.amazon.com/stores/Mary-A.-Couch/author/B07C5N7RLC, and https://whispersinthewind333.blogspot.com/search?q=couch, among other platforms and websites.

Bill Cushing *was* called the "blue collar poet" by classmates because of his years serving in the Navy and later working on commercial vessels before returning to school at 35, Bill Cushing's work has appeared in anthologies, journals, magazines, even newspapers. He has four previous poetry collections: *A Former Life* (Kops-Fetherling International Award), *Music Speaks* (San Gabriel Valley Poetry Festival Award; New York City Book Award), *". . .this just in. . ."*, and *Just a Little Cage of Bone,* his latest from Southern Arizona Press. He is working with that same publisher on two works planned for release before 2024: *Time Well Spent,* a collection of personal recollections, and *Two Brothers in the Civil War,* a historical narrative chapbook.

Paul Gilliland retired after over 30 years of service with the U.S. Army and settled in the high desert of Southeast Arizona, just miles from the historic wild west towns of Tombstone and Bisbee. He holds Associate of Applied Science Degrees in Intelligence Studies, Linguistics, and Education from Cochise College; a Bachelor of Arts Degree in Music Theory/Composition and Technical Theater Design from Olivet College; and a Master of Fine Arts Degree in Music Composition from the Vermont College of Fine Arts. He is an educator, composer of 21st century chamber music, author, form poet, publisher, and certified sound healer. He is a member of the American Society of Composers, Authors, and Publishers (ASCAP); National Writers Union; Authors Guild; Poetry Society of America; the Academy of American Poets; and the Association for Publishers for Special Sales. In addition to teaching interviewing techniques and report writing for the U.S. Army, he is the Editor-in-Chief of his own publishing company, Southern Arizona Press, and conducts light and sound therapy sessions to balance the chakras. He currently has four published volumes of poetry, *Hindsights of 2020*, *The Journey of the Fool: A Poetic Journey in Three Parts*, *A Heroic Crown and Other Sonnets*, and *Deeper Meanings* all available through Amazon or directly from him on the Southern Arizona Press website. He is currently working on completing his fifth collection of poetry, *Tales from a Southwest Inn* and a series of books based on his Master's thesis on the use of astrology and mathematics for the development of musical themes. His poetry has appeared online in numerous Facebook poetry group as well as being published in *Sonnet Sanctuary Anthology Volume 1*, (A Romeo Nation), *Open Skies Quarterly Volumes 4, 5, 6, Perceptions*, and *Dark Reflections*, (Shrouded Eye Press), and *From Sunset to Sunrise* (Dark Poetry Society Anthology) as well as occasionally appearing within the pages of the Southern Arizona Press poetic anthologies. He can be followed online at: https://www.facebook.com/PaulGillilandPoetry, https://www.facebook.com/SouthernArizonaPress, http://www.PaulGillilandMusic.com/, and https://www.SouthernArizonaPress.com/.

Kim Gwinner began writing about her pain and suffering from PTSD/MST in 2021 after beginning outpatient therapy at her local VA in Cincinnati, Ohio. Kim has since then published her first book *Healing Like A Warrior*. Kim currently lives in Walton, Kentucky. with her wife and pets. Kimmer is living her best life yet! https://www.amazon.com/stores/Kim-Gwinner/author/B0CDB1S9MJ

Chris Hasera is an American poet, veteran, and mechanic from Northern Indiana. He served three years with the 101st Airborne before re-enlisting with the 2123rd Transportation in the Kentucky National Guard. His printed words have appeared in *From the Edge of the Prairie, The Last Stanza Poetry Journal,* and *Ink to Paper* volume 6, as well as *december* magazine. He can be heard reading his own work on an episode of *The Storyworks Podcast.*

Lon Hodge, also known as Lonnie, is a disabled Veteran and retired professor of psychology and literature. He has been awarded fellowships and residencies by the NEA, the Texas Commission on Arts and Humanities, Illinois Arts Councils, the Millay Colony, Grand Marais Arts, and others. His work has been widely published and anthologized. His first book was the winner of the Sandstone Prize. He's written and produced two plays: *An Evening with William Butler Yeats* and A one-man show about Martin Luther. He is currently working on a play entitled *Mail Call* about letter sent to and from Soldiers during wartime. He's also the author of a collection of dog stories, a Colorado pictorial, and wild game cookbook among others. For the last nine years he has travelled the country with his service dog Gander and has divided himself between volunteer work with disabled Veterans with invisible disabilities, Veteran homelessness, service dog access, suicide prevention and planned acts of community kindness for those with invisible disabilities. In the last few years, he has raised money for other groups in excess of $3 million, performed dozens of acts of kindness, giving homeless and needy Vets tens of thousands of dollars of survival gear and adaptive equipment and has done over 300 seminars for police, fire, medical colleges, community groups, Fortune 500 companies and primary and secondary schools. He and his Service Dog have been the subject of documentaries, hallmark special, a PBS special, and dozens of news articles and television features. He was Medical Command Soldier-of-the-Year and an instructor at the Army's Academy of Sciences before going to Officer Candidate School and being commissioned as an Ordinance Officer. His last to the assignment was as Executive Officer of an ammunition plant. Lon's father served in both WWII and Vietnam. His father, wounded near Saigon in 1967 with only nine months left to retire, returned home and eventually succumbed to his wounds. He was one of the first nationally certified employee assistance professionals and he has worked extensively with police, fire and critical incident stress debriefing and counseling. He actively trains police and fire nationwide on service dog access and care particularly involving Veterans with PTSD. He holds degrees/certificates in Metallurgical Engineering, Communications, Asian Studies, Psychology, Counselor Education, and Creative Writing. His book, *In Dogs We Trust* is available at: https://www.amazon.com/Dogs-We-Trust-Unconditional-Inspiration-ebook/dp/B00FU9RDX8

Derrick Iozzio is an Army Veteran and former First Responder. Originally from New Jersey, Derrick enlisted out of high school and served in the Army for nine years. After being honorably discharged as a Staff Sergeant (E-6), Derrick went into civilian law enforcement and served for seventeen years. The experiences from the military and law enforcement were the foundation that caused Derrick to receive a degree in psychology and then become a state-certified Mental Health Peer Specialist. Derrick continues to serve, addressing mental health issues, the suicide crisis, and homelessness. Derrick facilitates Mental Health Peer Support Groups (in person and online). It is Derrick's hope that this book will help move the conversation and stigma surrounding mental health and suicide in a positive direction. There is a crisis, and to address that crisis, we have to talk about it, listen to others, and support them as they begin the recovery journey. Every one of us can do something, no degree is needed, and no special training is needed. We just have to be willing to listen, care and offer support. There is HOPE! There is HELP! Forever Forward!

Larry Murley was born four months before Hitler invaded Poland, during WWII. He grew up in a small farming community and watched the struggle of his parents and community during the War. Rationing affected everyone. Shortages of staples, sugar, coffee, and other items made people careful in their daily lives. He remembers gasoline stamps from that era, you couldn't just go driving for pleasure, those days. Then there were the casualties of war, everyone who had family abroad worried. In 1961 he received his Selective Service classification, he felt it his duty to serve. His Uncle spent the winter of 1944-45 in Ardennes, Germany, at the Battle of the Bulge. He decided he would join the Air Force, and see if he could get a leg up, and gain further education. At that time he was working in a Copper Mine in Arizona. He went through boot camp in fall of '61 and received overseas orders. He didn't know at the time he was headed to a little known place called Viet Nam, indeed, he had never heard of the place. He arrived in Viet Nam shortly after the first of the year in '62. Life changed for him then, his stay was short, but eventful. Viet Nam at that time was run by the CIA and the military part by MAAG-V. He spent time in the Central Highlands with the Montagnard people. In late April, his father was seriously injured, and the Red Cross spent nearly two weeks finding him. He was sent home immediately. He left Da Nang, South Viet Nam on May 13, 1962. He never forgot Viet Nam or its people, and now is associated with several Veterans groups. In 2012, he was having difficulty with it and his wife Kerry suggested he write his Viet Nam story. In 2014 he published, *Loss of Innocence, A Viet Nam War Story*. He has since published nine more books, and most of his books reference PTSD, regardless of what war they are about. In 2016 he became a member of MWSA, Military Writers Society of America. He became involved in the world of Renaissance in 1988, and in 1992 he and Kerry opened Crystal Mountain Oils and Incenses at the Awesome Texas Renaissance Festival. 2023 will be their 33rd year as shopkeepers there.

Gloria Nesloney served in the U.S. Marine Corps. She gave her heart to Jesus in 1995 and was called into ministry in 1998 when she began teaching at South Texas churches. She studied at International School of Ministry, Commission to Every Nation Missionary Program, and God's Living Words Ministries where she received her credentials as a Pastor and then a Doctor of Divinity. She is a student at Christian Leaders Institute. She conducted revivals, retreats; teaching, counseling, performing evangelical and missionary work in Texas, Mexico, Guatemala, Panama, and Uganda. She was involved in churches as a pastor, worship leader, administrator, Sunday School Teacher, and Council Member. She is involved in youth-adult ministries in church, on highways and byways, and online. She counsels those dealing with or overcoming addictions and helps families who need restoration. Her interests are spiritual warfare and victories through prayer and fasting, deliverance, healing, and the manifold gifts of Holy Spirit. She has a special interest in Women Veterans' inner healing and deliverance that have experienced PTSD, TBI, MST, suicide attempts, nightmares, or other traumatic events. She developed/led several Women's Ministries to help wounded warriors find hope. She founded a women's ministry group called S.T.E.P. UP as an online monthly challenge to grow in relationship with God, Jesus, and Holy Spirit. Gloria and her husband are currently serving the Church in the Coastal Bend area in South Texas. She has written books based on some of her experiences in ministry including: Author: *From Glory to Glory: Enraptured*; Author: *From Glory to Glory: The Dew Under the Leaf*; Author: *From Glory to Glory: In His Time*; Co-Author: *Veterans Unchained: Breaking the Chain of Trauma One Link at a Time*; Co-Author: *Let Go or Be Dragged: Experiencing Freedom from Negativity and Trauma*;

Co-Author: *Clinging to the Vine: Stories to Help You Draw Closer to the Lord*; Co-Author: *Return to Me: My Scars are Healed*; Featured Author: *Unexpected Blessings: Finding Joy*; Co-Author: *Veterans Unchained 2.0 - Lessons Learned*; Co-Author/Poet/Artist: *Kaleidoscope: Developing an Optimistic View of Life*; Co-Author: *Unexpected Blessings: Forgiveness.* #GloriaNesloney @glorianesloney. You can view her books here: https://www.amazon.com/stores/Gloria-Nesloney/author/B0B3BDGRWK, https://www.barnesandnoble.com/s/gloria%20nesloney.

Through Our Eyes was also compiled/written/edited by Courtenay Nold.

Courtenay Nold, LTJG, U.S. Navy, served just short of 15 years in the U.S. Navy and U.S. Navy Reserve (2000-2014). She was an enlisted Yeoman (former Chief Petty Officer/E7) and a Limited Duty Officer Lieutenant Junior Grade (O2). She cares deeply for others, especially those who, like her, have dealt with PTSD and Moral Injuries. Along with her focus on changing lives, Courtenay is an accomplished writer and poet. She has contributed articles to the Association of the United States Navy (AUSN) *NAVY Magazine* and *AT EASE! Veteran's Magazine*. She is a featured author and poet in the anthology *Veterans Unchained*, a #1 Amazon Bestseller, published in 2022. She also had poems included in *Father,* a Poetry Society of Indiana Publication. She published her first book of poetry via Southern Arizona Press, titled *Removing Interference: From Words of Life*, available from Amazon at: https://www.amazon.com/Removing-Interference-Words-

Courtenay-Nold/dp/1960038303 or directly from the publisher at https://www.southernarizonapress.com/store/Removing-Interference--From-Words-of-Life-p571439759. Courtenay holds a B.S. in Organizational Security and Management and is also a Certified Paralegal. She organized alternative therapies for PTSD book titled *Total War on PTSD* available on Amazon, Barnes and Noble and via Southern Arizona Press here https://www.southernarizonapress.com /store/Total-War-on-PTSD-p585724294. She regularly publishes her poems on the Poetry Society of Indiana's Facebook page at: https://www.facebook.com/PoetrySocietyIN. She also writes poetry on and curates/administers her Poetry Warrior page at https://www.facebook.com/groups /945323226710286. You can reach Courtenay directly at courtenaynold@att.net. Lastly, she had one of her poems published in the Fall 2023 edition of *At Ease!* Veterans Magazine, available at https://ateaseveteransmagazine.com.

Through Our Eyes was also compiled/written by Travis Partington.

Travis Partington grew up in the Midwest before moving with his family to the South. From there he joined. the Marine Corps and served as a Radar Operator for the HAWK Missile System. After the Marine Corps, Travis moved to the Boston area, and worked for a financial services firm. Travis is the host of the military and Veterans podcast, Oscar Mike Radio. This podcast has completed over 350 shows and is in the sixth year of production. In addition to using his voice for Veterans, Travis has also done voice-overs and is currently working on an audiobook *A Warriors Garden*, written by Malachias Gaskin. In 2022, Travis' contribution to the anthology, *Let Go or Be Dragged*, made Travis an International Bestseller. Travis has also contributed to *The Resilient Warrior*, *Born in a Bar 2*, and *Veterans Unchained 2.0*. Travis enjoys being a dad, the outdoors, archery, and riding his motorcycle. Being a father is the most rewarding aspect of Travis' life. You can go to www.travispartington.com or www.oscarmikeradio.com to see what Travis is doing and you can contact him at either site.

Teresa Pruitt submitted a poem as her bio.

I simply write for the pleasure and challenge
that I find in word expressions.
Not knowing, if my written words
will ever make if off the pages
and into a reader's mind.
As I write,
a quiet dream lives inside me.
In this tranquil dream,
my body is resting beneath a blanket of dirt.
The bemused human race still presses forward.
Magically, a future being
lays eyes upon my written words.
To this being,
the words are like finding
a treasure chest full of gold,
or a drifting bottle with a message inside.
The words become like footprints in the sand,
guiding and inspiring this future reader.
The reader absorbs the pages.
Pages written about my thoughts and feelings
of life's defeats and triumphs.
Then, as the reader
makes a connection to my written words,
once again,
a part of me lives.

Kate VerSluis, NC1(EAWS), U.S. Navy (1982-1994). Kate was born in Nevada and raised on a farm in Downsville, Wisconsin. At 19 she enlisted in the United States Navy, which provided an opportunity to enjoy the cultures of many different countries. She also earned her Enlisted Aviation Warfare Specialist. After the Gulf War, and 12 years of military service, Kate relocated to Sabattus, Maine, utilizing her Telecommunications Degree in the cable industry until retirement in 2014. Kate now spends her time enjoying art and adaptive sports. She sells her art through Facebook @whateverartbykate_versluis. All proceeds go to the Corey Edwin Garver American Legion Posts 202, Topsham, Maine to support local Veterans. For more information about American Legion Post 202, visit www.post202me.com/

Robert Willoughby, Psy. D. is a Doctor of Clinical Psychology trained at the Michigan School of Psychology. His dissertation, *A Heuristic Investigation of Private Ambulance Paramedics and EMTs*, investigated the work-related stressors, exposure to primary and secondary traumas, and personal and family impacts, including suicide of first responders. He currently works as a psychotherapist to children in community mental health and serves as the Care Pathways Program Manager which oversees the Zero Suicide Program and DBT style group services. He also works in a general private practice. Dr. Willoughby has given many presentations relating to PTSD in first responders, stress in first responders and emergency health care settings, suicide prevention and treatment, and an existential perspective of suicide. On a personal note, he is a dedicated husband and stepfather who enjoys cooking, hiking, arts, crafts, and video games.

Marilyn J. Wolf of Fishers, Indiana, has been writing since childhood. She is from a military family. Her great-great-grandfather fought in the Civil War after coming to America as a teenager. Her brother and his son are retired Army; his daughter-in-law and grandson are active-duty Army now. Her partner is retired Army. Internationally reviewed *In Celebration of the Death of Faeries* is her first chapbook. Her work has been published in *The Polk Street Review*, *Last Stanza Poetry Journal*, *Pebbles* Haiku journal, *Poet's Choice*, *The Elevation Review*, and *Living Artistically*; displayed in galleries at Nickel Plate Arts, Community Education Arts Online Showcase, Lost Dog Gallery, and the INverse Poetry Archive. She writes and edits regularly in a variety of publications on Medium.com as @Wolfen25. She is a member of local, state, and national poetry organizations, currently an editor of *The Howling Owl* and *Scrittura* on Medium, and past 1st VP of the Poetry Society of Indiana.

Pages for Reflection

Made in the USA
Coppell, TX
19 November 2023

24406628R00138